Now, tell it to me

Using Retelling for Literacy and Language Development

Mariellyn Hilgeman

Now, tell it to me

**Using Retelling
for Literacy and
Language Development**

By Mariellyn Hilgeman

© 2008 by Mariellyn Hilgeman

Purposeful Design Publications is the publishing division of the Association of Christian Schools International (ACSI) and is committed to the ministry of Christian school education, to enable Christian educators and schools worldwide to effectively prepare students for life. As the publisher of textbooks, trade books, and other educational resources within ACSI, Purposeful Design Publications strives to produce biblically sound materials that reflect Christian scholarship and stewardship and that address the identified needs of Christian schools around the world.

Unless otherwise identified, all Scripture quotations are taken from the New American Standard Bible (NASB), © 1960, 1962, 1963, 1968, 1971, 1972, 1973, 1975, 1977, 1995, 1997 by the Lockman Foundation.

Printed in the United States of America
14 13 12 11 10 09   2 3 4 5 6 7

Hilgeman, Mariellyn
    Now, tell it to me: Using retelling for literacy and language development
    ISBN 978-1-58331-094-6 Catalog #6585

Designer: Mike Riester
Editorial team: Karen Friesen, John Conaway

Purposeful Design Publications
A Division of ACSI
PO Box 65130 • Colorado Springs, CO 80962-5130
Customer Service: 800-367-0798 • www.acsi.org

Table of Contents

CHAPTER 1

Retelling Basics

Retelling and Blocks

When you remember kindergarten, what comes to mind? Dolls and dress-up clothes? Painting with a thick brush while being protected by your dad's old shirt that you're wearing backward? Sitting cross-legged on the floor listening to stories? Reaching for the sky with your toes as you pump higher and higher on the swings at recess? Building with those large, honey-colored wooden blocks?

Some things have changed. The jungle gym and teeter-totters have been replaced by forts. Parents no longer save boxes and cans for the house corner; instead, the children play with purchased play food that is realistic enough to make a person's mouth water. Dad's old shirt stays home, and children wear plastic aprons with a pocket in the front to catch drips during painting.

Some things have changed, but not all. Curious George, Madeline, and Little Sal share the library shelves with a host of delightful new friends. In the playground is an assortment of slides—traditional, corkscrew, covered—that wait together under the trees for recess.

Metallic colors, flesh tones, and fluorescent shades have joined but not replaced the red, yellow, green, and blue crayons in the box.

Some things continue to be popular year after year. Block areas have containers of brightly colored plastic blocks that invite children to come, snap them together, and create something. They come, they snap, and they create. But their most elaborate play, day after day, is with the simple, unpainted wooden blocks. Why? I think the reason lies in the blocks' simplicity and the nature of man.

- First, the blocks enable us to satisfy a fundamental human urge that links us to our Creator—the urge to express ourselves, to create something. Their very plainness offers greater scope for that creativity.

- Second, their stark simplicity gives them a flexibility that is lacking in more ornate blocks. Safety issues aside, there is no one "right" way to use them. We can lay them flat, stack them, set them up like dominoes, build a pretend boat to sit in or a garage to park our toy cars in—the possibilities go on and on. We feel we are in control.

- Related to this, almost anyone can use them and gain pleasure from the activity. A small child stacks two blocks and claps his hands in delight. An older child or adult takes pleasure in creating something more elaborate. Individual differences of all kinds are welcome in the block corner.

- Fourth, while in the process of constructing, children discover new things and delight in using those discoveries. They may gain the understanding involved in making a tower that incorporates space as an element of design. They may develop an appreciation of symmetry and balance. They may discover that they have the ability to problem solve, to work together with others, to persist at a task—we all enjoy trying something new and having it work, and then we tuck that knowledge under our belt for the next time.

- Fifth, the smooth surfaces and simple shapes please the senses. Remember those arches and columns? Remember the feel and heft of the longer blocks?

- Finally, and of value to teachers especially, they're nonconsumable. True, there is a considerable initial cost, but divided over the years of use, that cost becomes less significant. The blocks are virtually indestructible.

Retelling, along with blocks, has a long history of use in kindergarten. Perhaps teachers haven't always called it by that name. Perhaps they just asked, "Can you tell the story?" But they used the concept of retelling, and many continue to use it. Why? Again, I think the answer lies in the method's simplicity and the nature of man.

- First, part of the appeal of retelling rests in the universal, God-given urge to express ourselves and to learn about others through the way they express themselves. We're all unique, and we want to share that uniqueness with others—to know and to be known. We value children as a group, and we want to know them better as individuals.

- Second, there is no one "right" way to use retelling. The basic process can be used with large groups, small groups, pairs, or individuals. It can be guided or unguided. It can be verbal or nonverbal. It can be used with practically any subject. There are some ways that are more common than others, but we don't need to be limited to those. We can adapt retelling to our purposes and to our students' abilities and needs.

- Related to that, virtually anyone can retell a story at some level. Articles mention using retelling successfully in ESL classrooms, with students who have disabilities, with nonreaders, with readers of low and high proficiency, with very young children, and with adults. Retelling allows us to embrace individual differences with a minimum of effort.

- Fourth, as we use retelling, we realize that it reveals other facets of a child's understanding and thinking that a child's responses to specific questions miss. A combination of the two methods—retelling and a question-and-answer format—gives us a more complete picture of what a child knows and can do. At the same time, just as we learn and comprehend material better when we teach it, children comprehend and remember the material better when they retell it.

- Fifth, students enjoy retelling—although not always immediately because the task is unfamiliar to many children. Some children need time and support to develop language fluency, to become accustomed to focusing their attention during group time, and to learn to use story structure as a memory prompt. Eventually, however, most children take great pleasure in expressing themselves and in having their words preserved.

- Finally, retelling appeals to teachers because it is low in cost and simple to use. We don't have to buy something new before we ask children to retell a story. We don't have to make elaborate preparations in order to implement retelling.

When stripped to the barest essentials, retelling consists of input and output. Most commonly, retelling is used as a child's response (either oral or written) to literature that is either *told to* or *read to* that child—or, in the case of an older child, *read by* the child. That was my starting point. Yet, because my students were young and many were coping with learning a new language and culture, I began adding observations and experiences to input and nonverbal expression to output.

Background for the Examples

I taught kindergarten overseas for a number of years in a school that existed to offer education to the children of missionaries and other expatriate families. If there was room, children of the host country were admitted—children whose English was strong enough to profit from immersion in an American school. It was a young school, and we were blessed with a director who had enough confidence in his teachers to allow us a great deal of freedom.

Near the end of my fourth year, when I was planning a Bible unit and casting around for an activity besides what the teacher manual offered, I came up with a wonderful new (at least to me) idea. The students would individually retell the story, I would type their retellings, they would illustrate the text, and each child's retellings would be fastened together to create individual books for each of their stories. I had hopes that this would be immeasurably more interesting than gluing cotton balls on pictures of sheep on a mimeographed page. And it was.

We had one computer in the school in those days—in the office next to the playground. I used my recess break to type each child's story as the child retold it. I started with two children; when the first child finished and returned to recess, that child sent another child in. By the time the other child arrived, the second child was almost finished and ready to leave. Everything worked smoothly except for one complication: I never expected the children to retell the stories with such detail. Partway through the first session, I realized that there was no way I'd be able to get all the stories done before my aide left. Cotton balls and sheep began to sound more reasonable. All ended well, however, thanks to the school secretary, who agreed to watch my students at recess while I finished the last two stories.

At this point, I would have heaved a sigh of relief and vowed never to do another retelling except for the fact that I was hooked. As my children retold the stories, I became fascinated by their mistakes. There were parts that they interpreted by changing the parts to make sense with what they knew of life, and they retold each story in a way that was distinctly "kindergarten" in tone and language. I decided that this activity was worth the time and effort.

The examples of retellings in this book are drawn from twelve years of retellings by kindergarten classes at that school. Most are Bible stories. Gradually I branched out and began using retelling in other parts of the curriculum as well. The level of English may seem low to you, but keep in mind that for many of these children, English was a second or third language. When they left school they heard and spoke Spanish, Japanese, or Korean the rest of the day. I also typed the stories exactly as they were told to me, without cleaning up the pronunciation or grammar; thus I had a record of their progress in English.

Among these kindergartners, only a few native English speakers with strong backgrounds in Bible stories ever wanted to polish their work by rewording something. Occasionally, in a group retelling, some children suggested a different way to say something, but again, this was not common. That any kindergartner would want to do this took me by surprise that first year. Michelle, whose story follows, would often stop herself in the middle of a retelling to ask me to read back her last sentence, and then she would change the wording slightly until she was happy with it. Alerted by that, I began reading aloud the children's retellings and each class retelling when the children announced that they were done, and then I asked whether they wanted to change anything. Rarely did they say yes, but I continued the practice primarily to emphasize that their words had been captured with the letters they were learning and that those words could be read and treasured.

The attraction that held me, that kept me returning to retelling year after year despite the time involved, was what I learned about my children and their perspectives. The glimpses into each child's thinking and uniqueness fascinated me. Some children displayed a bent toward expressive storytelling. Others went straight to the facts and retold them succinctly. Some could not recall much of anything near the beginning of the year, while others overflowed with description and dialogue from their first retelling on. Some who had no previous experience with Bible stories confused names, characters, and stories when they retold: "Moses was a real bad king. He said, 'Yes, throw the baby boys in the reeber.'" Sometimes ideas from who-knows-where found their way into stories: "The king sent 'is messenger to tell the people they had to go England and Mary and Joseph knowed it's a long trip." I learned how to modify my storytelling and to better support children's learning as time went by, but the charm of my students' retellings was that they never sounded exactly like my story. Every story retelling session was a discovery.

The following are two stories from the first year:

David and King Saul
By Roberto[1]

When Dabid kill the giant Goliat, the people start to sing songs of Dabid and start to said Dabid is a stronger. When Dabid go to King Saul, King Saul is angry and he start to throw things. And David want to play beautiful music for the king and King Saul throw a spear for David. And Dabid run away of his kingdom. And Dabid have a specially friend, is son of the king. And he said, "I know you going to be the king next of King Saul." And the son of King Saul not start to be angry because David going to be king next and he said, "I want to be your much help when you got to be the king." And the son of King Saul go to see and he say, "You no going to kill David, he you soldier, he love you." He throw a spear. He go a David and say, "You go a forest and stay out of a king."

David and King Saul
By Michelle

Once there was a king long, long ago. His name was Saul. And he got very mad one time—he even tried to kill his own son, he was so mad. This is how it began. David had killed Goliath so everybody was saying good things about David like "David's the bravest, David's the strongest, David's the best" so King Saul got very jealous and mad. And

---

1 All children's names have been changed, but the stories were recorded exactly as the children told them.

David went to play some music for him as he had done before because David loved the king. But instead of the king getting happy, he got mad. And he threw a spear at David. So David didn't wait to get thrown at again, he ran out of the palace. And he had made a enemy, but God also gave him a friend. Jonathan the king's son was there, the prince. "I will go tell my father not to be mad at you anymore." He went and said, "Father, this is not right to be mad at him." And King Saul just threw a spear at Jonathan. So Jonathan just ran and said, "David, I can't help my father, the king." And Jonathan said, "Run and hide, David. David, you will be the next king even though I am the king's son. I will be your very best helper."

CHAPTER 2

The Retelling Process

Sometimes when I need to learn about a new topic, I go to the children's section of the library and read a book on that subject, thus getting a general overview—often complete with pictures and diagrams—before I start wading through more detailed adult books on the subject. This system, which works similarly to the way D. P. Ausubel's (1960) advance organizer works, gives me the basic hooks on which to hang information so that I don't get lost in the details.

Before we turn to specifics about input and output, let me paint two word pictures of retellings to help those who are less familiar with retelling put in place the details that follow. In the first word picture, which involved a group retelling, students used information from a number of sources to create books. The second, which involved individual retellings, is a more detailed account of the process I followed in recording individual retellings.

Spiders (A Group Retelling)

Because we were part of a school that included all grades—elementary through high school—the preschool and primary classes did class projects whenever the big kids had a science fair. The first step in the class project was to pick a topic of interest. This particular year, after several years of doing projects that had required the trapping of food or the opening of windows occasionally to air out the room when something had died after we'd left for the day,[1] I decided that it was time to do a project on leaves.

When I suggested this project to my class of ten boys and two girls, the girls were fine with the idea. Throw in a few flowers, and they'd be perfectly happy. The boys, on the other hand, protested, "Leaves? No way! We want to do spiders." The only spider I've ever warmed up to is Charlotte. But since (a) the vote was ten to three, including my vote of course, (b) it really didn't matter that much, and (c) I heard one boy whisper excitedly, "Hey, I've got a better idea! Let's ask her if we can do snakes instead!" we did spiders. The condition for this (similar to the laws of the Medes and the Persians) was that all spiders brought to school for study had to be in jars with lids securely closed at all times. The air holes had to be smaller than the arachnid within. And the spiders had to be taken back home each day after their three hours of fame at school. This settled, every day thereafter, you could see kindergartners on the school bus clutching clear glass jars with trapped treasures. Spiders should be on every list of Bolivia's abundant natural resources; we rarely had any duplication.

We used magnifying glasses to examine the spiders. The librarian sent us picture books of spiders, most of which pictured North American spiders rather than South American ones. A book about how an orb spider builds its web sparked interest in the different kinds of webs and the marvel of spider silk. I found a video on spiders. The high school

---

[1] Earthworms decompose overnight when the soil in their jar is too wet. A large quantity of decomposed earthworms requires massive amounts of air freshener and all windows open to make the room bearable.

science teacher invited us to come see his tarantula. I flipped through my husband's books on spiders and insects to find the name of each new "guest" and interesting facts about it. When we discovered from one book that spiders have multiple eyes, we turned our magnifying glasses on a wolf spider, that day's catch, in hopes of seeing all its eyes when the light glinted on them.

After the children had observed the spider of the day, I told them what I'd been able to find in the guides we had. Although this "quick and dirty" explanation lacked the precision and polish of a book text, it held their interest. Afterward, I asked the group to tell me what they thought we should share with others about their spider. I wrote their comments on the board while they watched, to give them practice in reading readiness skills, and then I read it back to them, asking if they wanted to add or change anything.[2] While they were eating their snack, I typed what they'd shared, attached it to a page that had a large jar outline on it, and made copies for each child. During small-group time, with the jar containing the spider in front of them and magnifying glasses available, each child carefully drew a picture of the spider (inside the jar outline on their paper and below the information they'd dictated). By the end of the project, they each had their own book, created by them both as a group (the text) and individually (the illustrations), about different spiders in our area. When the parents came for the science fair, the students showed their own book and answered questions.

---

[2] If I were doing this project again, in addition to the writing, I'd add videotaping. I'd enlist the help of a parent or an older student as a camera person and then, pretending to be a TV reporter, I would stick a cylinder-shaped block (or similar "microphone") in the students' faces and ask them, as the experts, to share with our viewing audience something about this spider.

2

Had I planned ahead, I would have saved these retellings to share with you. Instead, I have two examples of group stories from an earlier year, this time about insects. In comparing the two stories, you'll notice that in the one about a firefly, the students referred to outside information, and in the second, about a praying mantis, they were more interested in describing what they'd observed. We never did get around to doing a project on leaves. Alas, perhaps we should have....

Firefly

It is a soft beetle. We don't know how it makes its light. Its light is cold instead of hot like other lights. When they are making the light they are calling boyfriends. That's backwards from people because boys call girls.[3] There is another bug that has the same kind of light and it will blink on and on until the firefly comes and then it eats it. That's really sneaky!

Praying Mantis

He is green and white and brown. He has like a kind of eyes on his back but it's not a real eye, it just looks like one. He knows how to fly. His head can turn so he looks behind him. He is the only insect that can do that. He eats other insects and other praying mantises. He has eyes like black dots. He has a long neck but shorter than a giraffe's. His antennae are shorter than his body, but they are long. His head is like a triangle. He has spikey things on his feet. His front feet can go up in the air like he's praying but not with the palms together. He looks like a plant. There are green and brown praying mantises.

---

[3] This retelling was done a long time ago, when it was considered less appropriate for girls to call boys on the telephone.

The Christmas Story (Individual Retellings)

Every year, we made storybooks of the Christmas story during the four weeks between Thanksgiving and Christmas vacations. Our Bible curriculum divided the story into six smaller stories, so we did two a week. In this case, a large percentage of the class was already familiar with much of the story.

The first year, in an attempt to keep the pages in order and reasonably clean (a goal that wasn't easily attained because we did this activity after recess), I gave each child a blank sheet of paper every time instead of several pages in booklet form all at once. And then at the end of the project, I stapled the loose pages of the book together. After a year or two of doing it this way, I decided to assemble the blank books beforehand because I wanted to emphasize that each story was part of a larger story, a book that the children were writing. For the first two stories I trustingly opened the book to the correct page when I handed it to them. By the third story I had discovered the wisdom in paper-clipping that page open. Presenting the children with blank books that begged to be filled was a risk, but it set the task apart from everyday coloring, gave a more convincing book appearance, and prevented last-minute sorting and stapling.

Early in the school day, I either read the story to the class or told it using flannelgraph figures. (The one year that I didn't use visuals, the stories tended to be less rich in detail and description.) We reviewed the story briefly. An hour or so later during small-group/center time, a group of four or five children joined me. The students each illustrated the day's story with markers or oil pastels while waiting their turn to individually retell it to me at the computer a few feet away. If I started

2

with the strongest storyteller in the group, by the time I got to the weakest, that child had been given the opportunity to hear the story several times.

I typed each retelling exactly as the children dictated it, trying to preserve their language, since to me that is part of the charm of a retelling. (For those who have never tried doing this, trust me when I say that it is much harder than typing in Standard English. But if you get it right, it sounds exactly like the child's rendition when it is read back.) After the students had left for the day, I cut my printed page of stories into individual stories. Then I glued each child's story to that child's illustration.

When all six stories were done, the children decorated the cover, and we added an "About the Author" page with the child's photo on it. During the last week, after asking permission from each author, I read the books aloud and commented on their illustrations, using all the expression and respect given a regular book. Some children squirmed and grinned in delight, while others just smiled calmly; they were all authors and they had books to prove it. Finally, they wrapped the books and took them home to their parents as a Christmas present.

Several years after I'd had one particular child in my kindergarten class, her parent told me, "One of our favorite Christmas traditions is to read Marcie's Christmas storybook aloud every year." It made me wish that I'd started this when my own children were in kindergarten, because I agree with her—Marcie's story is charming. (If you have trouble reading it, substitute r's for the w's.)

The Christmas Story
By Marcie

The angel Gabwiel came to Mawy an' said, "Do not be scawd. You awe gonna have a baby bown in Nazaweth." En the angel said, "I will tell Joseph too."

A angel that God had sended down fwom heaven told Joseph, "Take cawe of Mawy fow she is gonna have a baby en take hew to youw house." An' then Joseph woke up and he went and mawied Mawy.

One day Joseph came home calling, "Mawy, Mawy, we hafta go back to the place that thewe wewe bown. We will have to take a twip to Bethlehem. I'm sowwy, Mawy." But Mawy said, "God will take cawe of us." En the next day they stawted packing. And then they stawted. An' when they got thewe they knocked at the fust doow an' the innkeepew came out. An' Joseph asked, "Can we please have a woom?" An' the innkeeper said, "No, thewe's no woom in my place." An' they knocked at the next doow. An' asked, "Can we please have a woom?" And the innkeepew said, "No," and Joseph said, "Lookit my wife. She is tiewed." An' the innkeepew looked at his wife en he felt sowwy fow hew. En he said, "Thewe's a stable out back whewe people keep thew donkey. You may sleep thewe." An' Joseph said, "Thank you vewy much."

En Mawy had a baby. En they laid him in a mangew. En Joseph an' Mawy went to bed an the hay.

Shepuds wewe watching ovo thu flock an' a bwight light came an' the angel said to them, "Feaw not for I bwing you gweat tidings of joy. Fow thewe is a baby bown in Bethlehem. You shall find him wapped in swaddling clothes laying in a mangew." Mawy an' Joseph didn't expect

17

2

that company would come in the middle of the night. In they went to the stable an' found baby Jesus just as the angel had said. En they wooshipped Him.

Thewe wewe thwee wise men an' dey watched staws. En one of um found a new one. En he went to tell the othews, and they said it must be the hint a about a new Hebwew king. En they packed up thu camels. An the staw seemed to be wight ovew the house. En they stopped in Dawusalem to ask the king Hawod. En he said, "A new baby king? I'm the king." And he put a smile on his face to fool them. And he said, "When you find the baby, bwing him to me. Fow I too want ta give a pwesent to him too." An' they asked evwybody in Bethlehem if they could see the new baby boy. En they said, "You go in ta that house. That is whewe he is." En Mawy en Joseph wewe happy when they saw that the wise men wewe giving thu baby gifts.

Input: Preparation and the Choice of Materials

3

Retelling begins with input. From the last chapter, you know that input can be quite varied. For instance, the input for the spider project came from a number of sources—observation, books, teacher-given information, and videos—which children combined in their retellings. (Think of it as the forerunner of the reports children will be responsible for writing throughout their school years.) In the Christmas story example, input came from a story that was told by the teacher. In early education we tend to use stories with children; as a result, most of us associate retelling with narrative writings. However, to limit ourselves to using stories alone keeps us from considering many other possibilities. This chapter considers language and background experience and the choice of materials to be used in retellings. Chapter 4 explores various means of input—printed materials, nonprint media, experts and field trips, and observations and experiences.

Preparation for Input

Hazel Brown and Brian Cambourne (1987), proponents of whole-language learning, stress that retelling should begin with immersion. When applied to early education, that means that we do our best to prepare children for the reading, listening, and retelling experience by providing instruction in the areas of story language and background information and experiences.

Language

By the time they enter preschool, many children are familiar with stories and enjoy listening to them. As a result, they have become familiar with the language of stories. Why is this important? Research suggests that the language that children hear or read in books includes vocabulary that they are unlikely to hear in everyday conversation or on television. This is particularly true of Bible stories.

Donald P. Hayes and Margaret G. Ahrens (1988) compared the frequency of rare words used in books, television, and speech. (Rare words were those rated 10,000 or higher in frequency of use.) The listing of words that they used was a modified version of the *American Heritage Word Frequency Book* list published by researchers John B. Carroll, Peter Davies, and Barry Richman. These three researchers used 1,045 samples of published materials for grades three through nine, only 3 of which were religious education texts from a parochial school (Carroll, Davies, and Richman 1971; Richman 1971, xiii). Naturally, this limited representation of religious texts affected their rating of certain "rare" words, such as some from the Christmas story—*newborn* (10,156), *manger* (10,546), *shepherds* (10,856), *Bethlehem* (10,687), and *Jesus* (15,325). Even if the sampling is not ideal for preschool vocabulary, it still reminds us that some children are likely to be unfamiliar with such words.[1] Hayes and Ahrens (1988) found that preschool books used about the same number of rare words (16.3 per 1,000 words) as college graduates did in informal speech with friends (17.3 per 1,000 words). When adults talked to preschool children directly, the number of rare words dropped to 9.0 per 1,000 words. Remember how controlled Mr. Rogers' speech was on the television show *Mr. Rogers' Neighborhood?* The text for that show included only 2.0 rare words per 1,000 words. Using a greater number of less-common words exposes children to words like *grumbled, giggled, fingernails, earrings, unfair, penguin,* and *snack.* Balancing comfort and challenge is a never-ending task.

3

In some homes, however, the level of spoken English that a child is accustomed to hearing may be lower than Hayes and Ahrens' average. Over a two-and-a-half-year period for an hour each month, Betty Hart and Todd R. Risley (2003) studied the language heard by children in various families—13 professional, 23 working-class (10 middle-class and 13 lower-class), and 6 welfare. Hart and Risley began their language study when these children were from seven to nine months old. The average recorded vocabulary size for the adults in the three groups was 2,176 words (professional), 1,498 words (working-class), and 974 words (welfare). Combined with the statement by Hayes (2003) that 85 percent of adult conversation with preschool children in their samples relied on the 1,000 most common words in their list, this study of adult vocabulary suggests that some children are exposed to few rare words and are consequently less prepared to understand the vocabulary in the stories they hear in school. Although 1,000 words may sound like a small representation—and in one sense, it is—even 1,000 words can be a challenge if English is not

---

[1] For most of us in urban settings, *manger* is a rare word. I was fairly old before I realized that *manger* was not a synonym for *stable.* ("Away in a Manger" sounded like a place to me.) Thanks to well-illustrated storybooks, my three-year-old understood the connection between a manger and the Christmas story before he knew the word. During a walk through a pasture, he yelled, "Baby!" and took off running toward a feeding trough that he saw ahead. When a Spanish-speaking student of mine couldn't remember the word *manger,* she said that Mary laid Jesus "on da plate of da animals"—an interesting mental picture.

the language that parents know and use in the home. What about the other 15 percent of adult conversation with preschoolers? That part may include the key words in a story.

Children who are learning English as a foreign language may lack instant recognition of many common nouns and verbs and other parts of speech, and we as their teachers may not even realize it.[2] Use some of the following ideas or create your own to help these children build their listening and speaking vocabulary:

- Play picture lotto or bingo games (either commercially produced or teacher-created from extra workbooks) to give children the repeated practice they need for building instant recognition of common nouns.

- Use preschool picture dictionaries and word books. These help primarily with nouns, but sometimes they also include other parts of speech. Consider recording yourself reading such books for your classroom library. If the recorded books may be checked out for home use, other family members may benefit as well.

- Create a class book, picture wall, or PowerPoint presentation to help children learn verbs or other parts of speech. You choose the verbs, encourage the children to think of ways to show the action, and then have children volunteer to show that action while you take a picture or video. Allowing the children to take turns taking the pictures will probably result in some blurred and off-center photos, but there are times when participation trumps perfection.

---

[2] If you know a second or third language, estimate how many words you recognize and can use in that language. Apply some of the ideas from this section to that language to make you more sensitive to the difficulties of being in a classroom where you don't know the instructional language well.

By the time the project is done, everyone will have had plenty of practice with common verbs, prepositions, or any other part of speech you want to emphasize. Add extra challenge by doing the same activity in smaller groups to see if the whole group can guess the target word before the children in the small group reveal what they were portraying. Encourage children to make up sentences using the picture and word.

3

- Check your children's listening vocabulary of other common words as well, and teach these as necessary. Not knowing words such as *before, after, at, to, over, under, all, none, some, but, if, and, or, not, later,* and *now* can greatly affect a child's understanding of language. (See the Internet links in the appendix for vocabulary lists of common words.)

Before you tell a story to the whole group, give children who are learning the language a mental outline of the story by calling them to you and telling them the bare bones of the story at a slower pace using short sentences, simple vocabulary, verbal and facial expression, gestures, and pictures. The mental outline combined with the introduction or review of key vocabulary words enables listeners to fill in the unknowns they encounter with educated guesses. For Bible stories, encourage parents to buy a good Bible storybook in the child's native language and to read that to their child.

For most native English speakers whom we teach, we need to remember that even if Hayes and Ahrens' figures are based on a less-than-perfect word frequency source for Christian preschools, the possibility still exists that there are a number of unfamiliar words in the picture books we read and the stories we tell. I'm reminded of an anecdote from the book *Becoming a Teacher of Young Children* (Lay-

Dopyera and Dopyera 1990, 139) about a kindergarten class whose parents were coming to a meeting in their children's classroom. "There was eager discussion of what various children thought parents would like to see when they came for the meeting…. However, when asked to take a note to their parents announcing the meeting, several children looked puzzled and asked, 'What's a parent?' Investigation showed that the children's meaning for the word *parent* ranged from 'some kind of teacher' to 'bigger kids like teenagers.' Only a few children were sure that a parent is a father or mother."

Once we're alerted to possible vocabulary gaps, we can help children form the habit of asking about the meaning of words by regularly asking them what words mean as we read or, if we know that a word is unknown, explaining it beforehand. Following are some examples:

- We may explain a new word by preparing the children for the word beforehand. Using the popular story *The Tale of Peter Rabbit* and my favorite phrase from it (Potter n.d., 33), we might say to the children, "In this story the birds will beg Peter to try harder. The story says that they 'implored him to exert himself.' *Implore* means to beg. *Exert* means to try harder. Can you show me what you might look like if you were imploring your mother to let you stay up later? What would you say if you were imploring your mother to let you go over to a friend's house? Name something heavy that you would have to exert yourself—try harder than normal—to lift? Can you think of something we do in kindergarten that is hard for you, that you have to exert yourself—try harder—to do?"

- As we read, if we notice puzzled looks, we may simply amplify the words by saying, for example, "They 'implored him to exert himself,' that is, they begged him to try harder. They said, 'Please, please try harder!' ' "

- If the lack of vocabulary won't greatly affect understanding, we may choose to wait until the end and then, between readings of the story, discuss new words with the children, asking them what they think particular words mean when they consider the context, and then build on their knowledge.

Naturally, the more we read to them and encourage them to listen to cassette/book sets of picture books, the better. We can also encourage parents, particularly immigrant parents who may not have grown up with public libraries, to become familiar with their local library and the programs and resources—story hours, taped book sets, videos of picture-book readings and animations—that it offers young children.

Background Information and Experience

Supplying background information or experience that is lacking can be straightforward, such as in helping children understand different housing situations. ("Abraham and Sarah lived in a tent like this one. How would your life be different if you lived in a tent instead of a house?") On the other hand, most of us struggle at times to understand parts of the Bible—its figures of speech, the actions of individuals—because of cultural differences. As adults, most of us have a certain amount of background information, gained over the years, to draw on. Young children with little or no church background have to contend with the unfamiliar vocabulary and customs of Bible times. One child, aware that her parents didn't go to church or read the Bible, was concerned that they would not understand her story. She attempted to prepare them for her retelling of the Christmas story by beginning, "A very, very long time ago there lived humans an' they wore different clothes." Another example involves the sacrificial system, which is somewhat familiar to most adults, even though it is foreign to our culture. To young children who are hearing it for the first time though, it can be extremely puzzling. After hearing the story of Cain and Abel, those in the class who either were from a Christian home or had been in the school for a year retold it with some degree of understanding. There was, however, one child who was new to the school. She was encountering information about God and the Bible for the first time. She solemnly assured me that the reason God didn't like Cain's sacrifice was that He felt that people should eat their own vegetables (rather than pass them off on Him).

A child's experiences, and even lack of experiences, also affect how well the child will understand input. During my eldest son's preschool years, we lived in South America in a hot, dry, rural area with one paved road on which cars and trucks passed from time to time. A big city, highways, a toy store, TV, snow and sledding—all these things were missing from his "experience bank." My attempt to explain snow by using the buildup of frost in the freezer certainly left a lot to be desired, but sometimes all we can do is explain, show pictures, or demonstrate because giving children the actual experience is not possible. If the story or content is too removed from what children know, or if the vocabulary is overwhelming, children (or any of us, for that matter) struggle to make sense of the input. Rather than understanding the whole message or concept, they latch onto isolated bits and pieces or retain nothing at all.

Before reading to children, we usually spend time drawing out their knowledge about the subject by telling students the title of the book and asking them to predict what the text will include on the basis of that title. This type of class discussion pools knowledge from various students, and introduces or reviews vocabulary and content that they might expect to hear in the book. It also nudges their minds in the direction the story will be taking. All this facilitates listening comprehension and retelling, particularly for children who lack the background for that subject matter. Spending the extra minutes to prepare children before providing input may not prepare everyone completely, but it is still time well spent.

Factors That Make Material Easy to Retell

Malcolm Gladwell (2000, 25) coined the expression "stickiness factor"—that is, what there is about something that makes it stick with people. He observed that often the deciding factors in whether or not something becomes popular or is memorable are the result of "relatively simple changes in the presentation and structuring of information that can make a big difference in how much of an impact it makes." In the context of input, what factors can we tinker with to make a story or information easier to recall and retell?

Structure

First, excellent structure makes material easier to recall. Charlotte Mason (1989), a British educator around the turn of the twentieth century, relied strongly on narration as an educational method. Beginning when their students were first graders, teachers in Mason's school read aloud material that was "of a sufficiently literary character" (172), stopping after each paragraph or passage to ask children to retell what they had just heard. (The length of material and method of retelling changed as the children passed from grade to grade.) The teacher insisted on a single reading or hearing of the input in order to help the students develop their memorization skills and learn to pay attention. This discipline was dependent on the use of well-written material. (See the appendix to access an online version of Mason's book.)

An amusing recollection by Jean Mandler (1983, 20) about how she came to do research on story structure also emphasizes its importance. She writes, "I was familiar with Piaget's claim that children have difficulty in recalling stories in their proper order. From my observation of children, this finding seemed odd. The clue as to what might be wrong came when I examined the stories he had used. I tried to retell one of them one day and botched it. This (not surprisingly) suggested to me that there was something odd about the story, not the child."

Why is good structure so crucial? First, it enables us to understand and make sense of the input we are receiving. Gordon H. Bower (1976) likens awareness of story structure to knowing the rules (structural underpinnings) of a sport you are watching. During the Olympics, some newspapers will helpfully include information about the rules and scoring of events to encourage us to watch them. If you don't know this information, you see action and you see decisions being made while you're watching the game or event, but it's all an incomprehensible jumble. Second, having a clearly understood structure allows us to organize and store what we see in meaningful chunks that facilitate retrieval of it later.

There are various types of structure. Repetitive structure using a simple rhyme and colors makes the story *Brown Bear, Brown Bear, What Do You See?* (Martin 1992), first published in 1967, a perennial favorite. *The Three Bears* (1965) is another classic whose predictable structure, based on size, makes it relatively easy to retell. Jon's recognition and use of the numerical structure inherent in the following Bible story enabled him to recall it fully:

David Is Anointed
By Jon

3

Once upon a time God told a man to go to Bethlehem and get another man and to give him one of his sons fer being a king and so the first bigger came and God said, "It's not this one." Den da second oldest one came and God said, "It's not this one." And the third biggest came and God said, "It's not this one," and the fourth one and God said, "It's not this one," then the five biggest child came and it wasn't that one and the six came and God said it wasn't that one and the seventh one came and it wasn't that one. So the man said, "Don't you have another baby?" And the other man said, "Yes," and they called the shepherd David and den David runned an' so den he said, "Dis one is it," so he get his horn and den he put soil on his head and den he turn 'to a king an' he was so happy.

Another type of structure that is reasonably easy to identify and recall presents readers with a main character who must solve a problem. Typically there are also supporting characters and episodes along the way, all of which are unlikely to appear in a young child's retelling. When vivid action or drama is part of the resolution, the story becomes even easier to recall, as demonstrated in the following story:

David and Goliath
By Ricky

One time David's father woke him up an' said, "Take some cheese to the war an' some bread to give to da brothers." An' den he went there an' then he gave those snacks to his brothers an' to da bosses of him of the war. At den he was going they saw a gian' an' nen he told King Saul dat he wanted to fight Goliath. Then 'e said, "It's okay but you're too small." Den David said, "Once a lion came to eat one of my sheep an' I killed the lion. An' then anodder time a bear came to eat my sheep." Then King Saul said, "Okay." So then he went to the river an' got five roun' stones den he went to Goliath an' said, "You come with me with sword, spear, an' shield." An' nen he said, "I come a name a Lord." An' nen he got one stone his sling an' put it in a slingshot an' trow it at Goliath an' then Goliath died.

The parable of the prodigal son (about the son who makes a wrong choice, realizes it, and returns to his father who loves him) is an example of both excellent structure and universal emotional appeal:

The Prodigal Son
By Jack

The boy an' his dad, he lived very good and they did all kinds of stuff but one day the boy said, "Give me all your money." The dad said, "Okay, I'll give you all my money," and he went away and one day he reached in his pocket to get money and there was no money in his pocket and he asked one of his friends to give him money and the friend said, "Nope, not even a bit." And so he went to jobs, for lots and lots of days, and a man finally said, "You can feed my pigs." And he was so hungry he wanted to eat the pig's food. And he went back home an' he took him lots of days but he traveled with nothing to eat. And finally he reached home and his dad said and he ran an' he hugged him and da boy said, "I don't think I want to be your son, I want to be your helper. And I'm sorry." "Shhhh," said the daddy. "Bring him some clothes and shoes and let's have a party and go kill fifteen cows." And they were okay.

Familiarity

3

This leads us to a second element that makes material easier to retell—familiarity. Stories with understandable, familiar content or situations hold attention and are easier to retell because, as Yetta M. Goodman (1982) points out, children find it easier to predict what will happen if they can identify with characters. She gives the example of Navajo children who found it much easier to identify with, understand, predict, and later recall details from a story that contained sheep and Navajo customs than from a story about a boy inventor.

If a story contains elements, such as vocabulary, that are beyond children's experience, the children tend to make the elements fit with what they know. We have all heard children turn a new name or term into something they already know, whether it makes sense or not. (I suppose at their age a great deal of life doesn't make sense—what is one more thing?)

- "And then the wise mens found the baby Jesus and gave the baby Jesus sense of money, gold, and then ..."

- "An' they tole the king, 'Where's the baby of the jewels?' "

- "And David took his slinky."

- "David took out his swing and put a rock in it."

31

- "And they put a crown of swords on Jesus."

- "And it was getting kind of late and so the people stop working on Jesus's body. The next day was the Saddest Day when nobody did any work. The people were all sad in church."

This also applies to situations. Because Juanito had taken part in communion at his church, his experience dictated how he retold the story of the Last Supper:

The Last Supper
By Juanito

One day Jesus needed a house for the Passover. And then Jesus went to da house and then Jesus he gives little pieces of bread to his disciples and he give da bread for remember Jesus. And then Jesus give him some Kool-Aid in those little glasses of the church. Then he give da Kool-Aid for he can remember Jesus. And den he, the disciples didn't understand. And then Jesus said to the disciples that he is gonna die.

In the following story, I'm not sure whether Tori's limited vocabulary or limited experience in wild animal living conditions affected the retelling she gave. (Did she mean "cave" rather than "cage," or did she picture some of the animals happily heading for zoos?):

Noah and the Ark
By Tori

Dat God told him to make a boat, how big to make it an' how tall of make it. So then he let the animals go in. So after the animals went in, the other people went in too. Den it rained and rained and rained and it rained and it rained an' the boat was on top of the rain. And God said it was time for the water to go down. And den it went down and down an' down an' down an' down an' when it went down it got stuck on a roof or something, on a mountain. He sent a bird out and it never came back so he sent the white one out and it never came back an' so it carried a branch to him. An' den it went dada thing went down an' God let all the animals out an' so did the other people. And then da other animals went to go live in cages and stuff whatever they wanted to live in. So den the other people lived somewhere they had to be.

Another factor—one related to familiarity with setting, language, and experience—that predicts success in the retelling of a particular story is familiarity with the story as a whole. This familiarity makes small pieces of the story, a new detail, or a particular wording stand out. When it comes to Bible stories, children who have heard the story numerous times have a head start in recalling all the details of it. Such is the case for Ginny, who authored the following story:

33

David and Goliath

By Ginny

One day David's father told David to take some food down to his brothers because his brothers were in the army of King Saul fighting against the Philistines. David said, "Yes, Dad." So he start going down to the where his brothers were. And as soon as they got there he looked for his brothers an' he found them an' they started eating but when they were done they heard the thing telling 'um ready to fight. Then they heard the army of the Philistines coming. They heard big stamps. It was from the big giant Goliath. An' David asked his brothers, "Isn't there anybody who wants to fight the giant?" His brothers said, "Nobody wants to fight with him." David went an' ast some other people, "Do you want to fight the giant?" "We don't want to." "If nobody wants to fight the giant," David said, "I will fight the giant. I will go an' ask King Saul if I can." So he went to ask King Saul. King Saul said, "David, you are too small to fight. You are only a little shepherd boy." David said, "I was watching my sheep an' a big lion came up an' tried to get my sheep. And I prayed to God an' God helped me to kill the lion. Another time a bear came up an' tried to get my sheep an' I asked God an' He helped me again kill the bear an' I think God will help me again to kill this giant Goliath." An' King Saul said, "Okay, you can put on my armor an' go out an' fight." But when David put the armor on it was too big for him so he told King Saul, "This is too big for me an' I'm used to jus' doing it in my own clothes, in my own stuff." An' so he took it off an' den he went outside an' took five smooth stones from the stream that was running by. Then he waited for Goliath to come an' when he came, Goliath said, "What do you think I am, a puppy?" David said, "You fight with a sword an' a spear but the Lord will help me to kill you." Then Goliath got mad an' started to take out his sword to kill him but David

34

put a stone in his sling an' made it go fast an' it went up an' hit Goliath on the head an' he fell down an' then David took his sword an' used it to chop off his head. An' when the Philistines saw that Goliath was dead they started to run an' the Israelites chased after them and got them away from their country.

Not having that head start doesn't mean that children won't be successful; they just need to give careful attention during the story and reviews. The following story was new to Sheila (as were all Bible stories), and although she didn't go into as much detail as Ginny did in her story, Sheila still retold it well:

The Fiery Furnace
By Sheila

There was three boys. They were sent to a country. There was a king there and he said, "I'm going to make a big statue that shines. And when the music plays, everybody has to bow down." But the boys didn't. And the king liked those boys and he gave them another chance. And the boys said, "We don't bow down to you like God. We bow to God." So the king send his soldiers to tie them up and throw them into the room of fire. And then the king saw that they were in the fire walking around and he said, "Wait a minute. Did we throw three guys into the room of fire?" And his soldiers said, "Yes." And the king knew that his God was there, that their God was there, that's what he said.

During individual retellings, I encouraged the rest of the students in the group to listen while coloring as their classmate retold the story. How successful it was to have them listen and color at the same time is questionable, although occasionally a child like Rony, struggling to remember a word (here the word was *hosanna*), would refer to the

35

previous child's story: "They said, 'Praise the Lord,' no, they said—what did Helen say? I don't remember." Over time the retellings by the students got better, but I suspect this was the result of their acceptance of the responsibility for listening more carefully when the story was first told and of their increased familiarity with the task.

Think back to Charlotte Mason's (1989) philosophy that only a single hearing or reading of material was permitted. This may seem unnecessarily rigorous. Most educators today allow multiple hearings or readings of the story before asking for a retelling. First, according to David Yaden (1988), this approach may encourage children to think more about the passage and to understand it more deeply. (Of course you may ask for the retelling and continue to review the material after the retelling. Presumably, understanding will improve; however, you won't be measuring it unless you do another retelling.) Second, ensuring success for everyone, or at least trying to, is part of our culture. We want people to enjoy "the thrill of victory" whenever possible. I'm not suggesting that this is wrong. On the other hand, paying careful attention to what is heard is an important skill, one learned over time. In the beginning, while we are building a foundation in language, confidence, and experience, allowing multiple hearings before asking for a retelling is helpful, but I think it is also important to gradually move children toward taking the responsibility for listening well the first time they hear information. It's a matter of sensitivity and balance.

Delivery

A third element that makes material easy to recall and retell is delivery. My mother loved books, and she was a champion storyteller and reader of stories. I assumed that everyone read stories with wonderful expression—at least I did until the night that our favorite neighbor babysat. Even now I remember how cheated I felt, how disappointed I was by the way she rushed through the story in monotone. Delivery is the pretty ribbon that ties structure and familiarity into a delightful whole.

Think of the various elements involved in delivery and how they emphasize points, hold attention, and assist in recall:

- *The voice*—its tone and volume, pacing, use of pauses, expressiveness, tempo
- *The body*—movement, gestures, expression, tension or lack of it
- *Aids*—simple or elaborate costumes, music, and props

The likelihood that children will be able to recall and retell material is increased when we ensure that material is well structured, that children are supported by familiar language and experiences, and that they are captivated by memorable delivery. And importantly, when we are speaking about Bible stories and their application to life, we do not want to forget the role of the Holy Spirit. We prepare technically and spiritually and we teach, telling stories the best we possibly can, because we know that we are responsible to do our part to the best of our ability. Ultimately, however, God is the one who makes His Word stick to the mind and heart and who changes a life.

CHAPTER 4

Input: Types of Material and Activities

Many types of materials can be used for input:

- *Books and other printed material.* Books (reference books, narrative and expository texts for children, adult books including teacher manuals) that are read or that are used as the source for shared information are the most common source of input. Other printed material choices include charts, pictures, maps, and recipes. Pictures in particular hold an important place in early education.

- *Nonprint media.* Resources such as the Internet, videotapes, audiotapes, DVDs, and PowerPoint presentations provide students and teachers with variety in presentation and content.

- *Experts and field trips.* Guest speakers and field trips can be either simply time fillers or valuable sources of input, even for young children. The value of these types of input depends on how the teacher takes advantage of each opportunity.

- *Observations and experiences.* Guided and unguided student observations and experiences are other valuable means of input in early education. Retelling helps children remember and understand what they have seen and done.

Books and Other Printed Material

Narrative or Expository Writing?

Children are more familiar with retelling a story, a narrative of some kind, than they are with retelling expository writing. The story can be fiction or nonfiction (a Bible story, a biography, a historical account, a "true life" account). For most of us, narrative stories are easier to recall and retell than are expository writings. Why is that?

Is it because our parents began reading stories to us before our first birthday? This explanation sounds fine, except that when I recall the books that I read to my children in their earliest ages, the books weren't stories; they were concept books. (These types of books show a picture of a ball, with the text "ball" beside it, or they show a picture of a cow, with text that reads, "The cow says moo.") We eventually got around to stories, but not until their vocabulary and attention span had increased.

Is it because life is a story, the sum of many smaller stories? Babies learn sequences of events during their first year of life. It could be argued that we get into the habit of paying attention to narratives because we experience narratives that have meaning in our lives from the very beginning.

Another possibility occurs to me. Is it just a matter of the experience with narratives or could it be that our brains are hardwired to notice and recall narratives? After all, narratives are about characters (generally people) and about relationships between those characters. Relationships are central to life—in this world and the next. We learn about life through interactions with others with whom we have a relationship. We learn about God and how to relate to Him in the context of human relationships. Could it be that a merciful and loving God created us so that the personalities, words, actions, and reactions of people hold our attention more readily than facts? Is it because we are made in the image of God and, as a result, we desire fellowship with others, even if that fellowship is abstract (as in a story) rather than concrete?

Whatever the reason, no one would deny that we're drawn to stories. Cultures throughout history have used them to pass on values and beliefs to adults and children. Does the popularity and accessibility of stories mean that information texts should be avoided in early education? I don't think so.

We noted that structure (particularly story structure), familiarity, and delivery make material easier to understand, recall, and retell. We are all familiar with children's curiosity about the world; information books can satisfy that desire to know and understand. At the same time we instinctively realize that we need to offer more support when we use expository texts with young children. Authors and publishers have attempted to make factual content more accessible by linking abstract information to children's interests and experiences and by combining factual content with narrative features such as using a problem/solution story structure rather than a descriptive one. Hitting the right balance between imparting information and making it engaging is a challenge to writers of nonfiction for young children.

These accommodations help, but the language in expository texts is usually more challenging than that in narratives, and the concepts and information are often new and densely packed. Some books for young children deal with this challenge by relying on superb photography or illustrations to fascinate children and clarify new vocabulary and concepts. Some use the clever technique of combining a very simple text with additional information that the teacher or parent may decide to read aloud or ignore, depending on the audience. In the book *From Egg to Chicken* by Robin Nelson, the text "A mother chicken lays eggs" is in large print. The smaller print gives additional information: "A female chicken is called a *hen*. A hen lays many eggs. Inside each egg is a baby chicken" (2003, 4, emphasis in original). Similarly, if we're limited to using a book whose text is beyond our children's ability to understand, all of us have skipped or summarized parts of the text while emphasizing the illustrations.

If the structure of a book is descriptive rather than narrative, you can use a graphic organizer that supports attention and recall by making the structure explicit for children. Tell children that you will be reading a book about a particular subject—for example, monkeys. Ask the children what topics they think the book will cover. They might suggest topics such as what the monkeys eat, where they live, and so on. Write these suggestions in question form on the chart and explain that as they listen they will probably learn the answers to these questions. Read the book to them, and then finish the chart together afterward.

Another possibility is to introduce the children to the table of contents and use it to guide listening, stopping after each chapter to retell. (Remember that Charlotte Mason's practice was to have children retell after each paragraph, perhaps equal to a page or a topic in many nonfiction picture books.) Is it necessary to read a whole book and retell all of it? One value that author and educator Nell K. Duke (2003) mentions in connection with information books is that children gain a broader understanding of using reading as a means of gaining information. A story must be read from start to finish, but an information book is different. For instance, let's say you want to focus on baby animals. Though you may refer to several books on different animals, you might use only the section of each that deals with animal offspring. In the process you model the use of the index, glossary, table of contents, and drawings.

To focus attention on vocabulary and background information and experiences, another possibility is to use the K-W-L chart created by Donna Ogle (Blachowicz and Ogle 2001, 108–11). Ask children the question, What do we already *know* about this topic? to get background information from them. Then, raise listening expectations by getting their responses to the question, What do we *want* to learn about it? Afterward, gather responses to the question, What have we *learned*?

Can children do retellings that are reasonably rich in detail without using prediction or a chart? Of course they can. The act of writing ideas, however, lays everything out concretely for children to see rather than having to rely on their memory, and it helps in the organization of that recall. This technique is particularly helpful if a great deal of new information is being shared. In such cases, without the reminders provided by written notes or pictures, children are more likely to focus solely on recalling content haphazardly rather than on retelling with style. (The "Praying Mantis" retelling in the second chapter would have been improved by this strategy.)

Another way to approach the use of expository texts, particularly if students do not have a great deal of experience with the topic, is to read a story about the topic first. The information embedded within the narrative structure becomes background information and provides general structure on the topic. Later, this narrative should be followed up with an information text to increase the students' knowledge.

Children are curious about their world; we all know that. Christian teachers want to satisfy that curiosity and foster an appreciation of the world while directing children's attention to God as the Creator and Sustainer of His world. Though they may not be written specifically from a biblical worldview, expository texts—whether created for young children or created for older readers and adapted by the teacher to fit her audience—not only satisfy children's thirst for knowledge but also give teachers the opportunity to model the process of integrating a secular text with faith in God. We all need a concrete base to understand abstract concepts. When one of our aims for children is that they become lifelong learners who can discover the hand of God anywhere in His creation, we need to show them how to do that. Of course, stories may be integrated with biblical truth too. Both types of literature—narrative and expository—should be part of our classrooms.

Storytelling or Story Reading?

Does it matter whether a story (or any input) is told to children or whether it is read to them? The answer to that question, as suggested by the research of Rebecca Isbell, Joseph Sobol, Liane Lindauer, and April Lowrance (2004) at East Tennessee State University, is that it depends on your goals. This research measured language complexity and comprehension in preschool children after the children heard a story either told or read to them. There were some differences. When the story was told to them, children paid attention better and demonstrated better comprehension afterward, a result that makes sense as we think of delivery, eye contact, and the freedom to adapt a story to the listeners. When the story was read to them, the children showed more language complexity in their retellings. Since most of us speak less formally than we write, this also makes sense. The researchers concluded that both techniques are important since they each meet different needs.

Do these findings mean that you have to resign yourself to receiving less rapt attention and comprehension from your students if your preference is to read to them rather than tell them stories? Of course not. But while reading a story, keep the strengths of storytelling in mind. Work at using more eye contact and greater expressiveness, and offering explanations as you read. If your preference is to tell stories, plan the vocabulary carefully. Consider reading aloud book versions of the same story later in the week to introduce additional vocabulary.

Storytelling, at least really good storytelling, is not easy. When you read a book aloud, the story is given to you. The author has completed the preparation steps—those of structuring the story well, using a slightly broader range of vocabulary, and providing a captivating introduction, a challenging application, and a satisfying conclusion. When you tell a story, these steps of preparation, along with preparing children for the broader vocabulary, is your responsibility. If you are rushed for time, you may be tempted to skimp here. There may be truth in the matter-of-fact statement by Marie L. Shedlock (1917, 15): "So many storytellers are satisfied with cheap results, and most audiences are not critical enough to encourage a high standard." But should that statement be true—especially in a Christian school? Shedlock wrote that elements of delivery, such as gestures, changes in tone and volume, and, particularly, using pauses effectively, should not be left to chance. This is similar to the advice of another skilled storyteller, Ethel Barrett (1960), who also urges storytellers to prepare thoroughly, using atlases, commentaries, dictionaries, primary texts, and retellings of the primary text. An aura of authority and a sense of depth are based on a confident knowledge of the story details and background information, even if that information is not included in the story.

Another important caution, particularly as we deal with telling Bible stories to children, is that sometimes the medium overshadows the message. Barrett (1960, 56) writes, "In our desire to compete with the excitement of this wonderful world, we are apt to go overboard and dress up our Bible stories until they are out-of-bounds—and with the best intentions, we can be flippant with the Word of God." The excitement and gratification of holding children's attention can easily sidetrack us from the reason we are telling the story in the first place. She writes that the Holy Spirit is the one who will check us when necessary. During college, when I was assigned the telling of a particularly exciting, suspenseful missionary story during Vacation Bible School one year, I was brought up short and forced to reevaluate my purpose in storytelling when I overheard the children calling it the mystery story rather than the missionary story.

When Shedlock (1917) was asked whether children should answer questions, retell, or draw a picture of the story immediately after hearing it, she answered that they should not. A story (performance) should be followed by silence for a few minutes to let it have its effect on children. When compared to the storyteller's art, she explained, any efforts on the part of the children to reproduce the story immediately will only produce dissatisfaction for them. I doubt that most of us reach such performance heights that our young listeners will be overcome by feelings of inferiority, but Shedlock raises an important point regarding the retelling of Bible stories.

Our primary goal in telling Bible stories is to move children toward a personal relationship with God rather than simply to increase their biblical knowledge base. That relationship is anchored by knowledge of revealed truth (in His Word), but it goes beyond that. Emotion is involved. Perhaps a storytelling benefit, along with those of greater attention and comprehension found by Isbell, Sobol, Lindauer, and Lowrance, should be a deep emotional response inspired by stories told by one who is saturated with the message and with love for God and the children.

The Role of Visuals

4

Can you imagine early education without visual aids or pictures? We rely on them to help children bridge the gap between experience and new information and to help us teach more effectively (to capture wandering attention) and more efficiently (as the saying goes, "a picture is worth a thousand words"). Using visuals such as flannelgraph figures or pictures brings together storytelling's expressiveness and story reading's graphics, and is thus particularly helpful for students who are learning new vocabulary.

Because part of the story or message is being conveyed visually, the quality and accuracy of the visuals are important. One example that comes to my mind is a picture of the Annunciation in a coloring book. In the picture, Mary is reading a book (rather than a scroll), and the angel is carrying a flower. I realize that the Bible doesn't say anything one way or the other about a flower; however, both the flower and the book are likely to be recalled because they are concrete, familiar images. I feel quite sure that if I used that illustration while telling about Mary and the angel, I would hear several versions of "Mary was sitting in her house reading a book. An angel came to see her. He gave her a rose."

When I told the Creation story, I used a set of seven pictures, one for each day of the week. The first six pictures showed what God had created on those days, but the seventh picture was of a church, to signify that the seventh day is a day set apart for God. I noticed the break in the pattern of showing what God had created each day and assumed that my words would take care of it. When I told the class about the seventh day, I spoke about God resting, not because He was tired but because He had finished creating the world. I said that we celebrate that by going to church and worshipping Him on Sundays. I never said that God created churches on the seventh day. Out of a class of thirteen students that year, seven of them—those who were the more mature learners, those who had heard the story before, and those whose native language was English—got the point. But the other six children followed the picture pattern and said that God created churches on the seventh day. After that I made a point each year of telling my students that this picture was *different* from the others, that it *didn't* show something God made, because the seventh day was different.

As children retell, you begin to look at visuals through their eyes. The figures of the wise men that I used with the following story retold by Carter showed them kneeling and offering their gifts:

The Wise Men
By Carter

The wise men brought gifts to baby Jesus. They got off their camels, and they prayed to baby Jesus.

I probably said that the Bible says they got off their camels, knelt down, and worshipped Him. Carter probably associated kneeling and worship with praying and summarized it. After that year, each time I used those figures, I commented that kneeling is a way of showing that you feel the other person is very important. The wise men were important grown-up men, but they realized how special baby Jesus was, and they showed it by kneeling and giving Him gifts.

Besides clarifying vocabulary, the use of flannelgraph figures in a story also adds action (through putting up figures, moving them, and taking them down) and an element of anticipation. (When will the next figure go up and what will it be?) Usually, when using flannelgraph figures, the teacher is the guardian of the figures. As a means of holding the children's attention, consider allowing the children to have a part in moving the figures. You won't want to do this with every story, but there are some "slow" stories with which this works quite well. At this point, you may be worrying about protecting the figures; after all, they are expensive and you want them to last. If you prepare the children for their part, most will be so delighted at the honor of being the guardian of a figure that they will treat it well. Try the following:

- Have everyone sit in a circle on the floor. Tell them to zip their mouth shut or "hold a bubble" in their mouth, put their hands behind their back, and close their eyes.

49

- Quickly lay a figure on the ground in front of each child. Tell the children to keep their hands glued together behind their back and open their eyes. (I know that some eyes are peeking, but if the children aren't supposed to talk and their hands are occupied, you should have a head start.) Explain that the figures should be handled very carefully and that the children may pick up their figure and look at it now.

- Give all the children a short time to examine the figures and then tell them to put the figures back on the floor in front of them and put their hands in their lap.

- Explain that when their figure is needed in the story, they may get up and put it on the board but that they need to keep their hands in their lap until then. (Suggestion: If you have a student who is extremely impulsive, give that child the *first* figure in the story.) Keep all the figures once they are used.

- As you tell the story, when you get to the point at which a figure needs to be put up, pause to give the child a chance to recognize that he has the necessary figure and give him time to get up and put it on the board. If a child doesn't realize that he has the needed figure, you may have to give a hint or two. ("We need Abraham, don't we? Abraham was a very *old* man in this story. Who has a very *old* man?")

Vary your visuals by making four large scene cards rather than using individual figures. Mount the scene cards on cardboard, laminate them, and attach a piece of Velcro to the back near the upper edge. Pair these cards with a plain, sturdy background board or stiff cardboard that has one long horizontal strip of Velcro stretching across the entire width of the board near the upper edge. As you tell the story, place the scenes in order from left to right and leave them until the end. To reinforce left-to-right progression, put a green dot, a star, or another reminder on the left side. (This board could also be used for counting, for alphabet sequences to give children practice in getting the letters of their name in order, for blending activities—anything you might be using one line of a pocket chart for now.)

Give your students a smaller version of the board and cards at the beginning to use during the story if having them won't be too distracting for your students. Otherwise, use this as a retelling activity afterward. In this case, either retell the story or let the children do it while they attach the cards in order at the right time. The Velcro helps children who have problems with small-muscle control, it provides structure, and it makes a delightful sound. Vary this by using clip-on, clear plastic name badges that hold story scenes securely enclosed with tape so that the children can clip them in left-to-right order onto a sheet of very heavy cardboard.

Another possibility for input is using wordless books or, in Mason's example, pictures. In this case, the teacher "reads" the pictures and then supplies the verbal text to go with the pictures. For variety or extra practice, send individual versions of the books home with a note to the parents suggesting that they ask the child to tell the story. For children to be able to do a retelling that is rich in details about a wordless book, the teacher needs to model how to draw a story from the pictures. First look through the book, thinking aloud as you look carefully at each picture, mining it for details. Start again, this time using the general story line and details to create a rich verbal retelling.

51

This assumes that the wordless book or set of pictures contains enough details to prompt more than a sentence for each picture. Charlotte Mason explains how she uses retelling successfully with art appreciation classes: "Children learn, not merely to see a picture but to look at it, taking in every detail. Then the picture is turned over and the children tell what they have seen—a dog driving a flock of sheep along a road but nobody with the dog. Ah, there is a boy lying down by the stream drinking. It is morning as you can see by the light so the sheep are being driven to pasture, and so on; nothing is left out.... there is enough for half an hour's talk" (1989, 214; emphasis in original).

Not all pictures are that detailed. My experience with kindergartners and coloring books that cover one topic or story is that many are not rich enough in detail to encourage students to say more than the bare minimum. Usually the text below the picture is quite sparse as well. Can you use such a book? Of course! It presents a wonderful teaching opportunity. Start by reading the line below each picture, but after a few dull moments, interrupt yourself. Exclaim that there is more, much more, to this story than that. Pull out your Bible (if this is a Bible story) and using it, read and tell the story with details and great expression. Refer to the picture as much as possible in the process. (If the picture shows Abraham on a camel, how did he get there? Climb up a ladder? Jump? How do people get on camels? Why not incorporate that into the telling?) When children are ready to retell, remind them that they can say just one short sentence about each picture or they can use the pictures to help them tell the story.

Model this process by using a nonfiction picture book. Some older books have one "stock" picture on each page and several lines of text. After reading the book, make up a short sentence about each picture, such as "This is a giraffe" (for a picture of a giraffe in its natural habitat).

"Giraffes have baby giraffes" (for a picture of mother giraffe and baby). Explain that you could just say that one short sentence, or you can add more detail. Read to them again what the book actually says on the page. Help children grasp the concept that pictures can be used in a way that is limiting or enabling. At the same time you may want to caution children to stick to the facts so that their retelling is correct.

Finally, even young children can learn to extract input from charts, maps, diagrams, recipes, and how-to directions (Brown and Cambourne 1987) if the materials are simple enough. In the beginning, you will explain the chart to children. Gradually they will learn to "read" simple charts on their own, but you still may wish to "talk through" the chart first to provide vocabulary and to model its use. Consider the following examples: a three-step recipe for making butter, a chart showing a basic place setting on a table, and a diagram of the steps necessary for constructing a simple block structure. Think of some of the vocabulary involved in these examples: ordinal numbers and time expressions (second, after, until), cardinal numbers (five, six, one), verbs (pour, lay, fold), nouns (cream, lid, fork), position words (above, left, beside), comparatives (longest, biggest, smaller), shapes (cylinder, triangle, cube), and on and on. If many of your students are learning English as a new language, allow them to act out and say the words several times with you as you point to the chart and explain it.

Nonprint Media

The plus of storytelling and story reading is the dynamic relationship between the speaker and the audience. Sometimes for variety or out of necessity, the teacher may decide to use some other means of

4

communication during the input phase of retelling. Some of the ideas in the following paragraphs are quite simple; others require more equipment and expertise.

Most teachers have used commercial book/cassette combinations, some that include a preliminary "let's look at the pictures together" section and others that simply read the story. Whether these book/ cassette combinations are the only input source or a supplemental one, they are a boon to English language learners and their families, providing them with controlled, spoken vocabulary that they can replay as often as desired. Teacher-made versions (you can record yourself when you initially tell or read the story) coupled with the book, flannelgraph figures, or finger puppets make a nice addition to your listening center. If you record yourself reading a book to the class, students can participate by making the "turn the page" signal on the tape. I usually let the class decide what to use as the signal. Sometimes they chose a cymbal or tone block from the rhythm band set, and sometimes words or even sounds from the text such as "meow" for *Millions of Cats* (Gag 1928) and "kuplink, kuplank, kuplunk" for *Blueberries for Sal* (McCloskey 1948). My students loved participating in the creation of such tapes, and they listened to them repeatedly.

Some public libraries offer online a wide range of videos, audiobooks, and digital books. If your classroom has an online connection, you can download these for a specified length of time. (At the end of the lending period, they can no longer be accessed.) Some publishers allow books to be copied to a CD; others do not give that permission to the borrower.

If you have access to a video camera, ask a friend to film you as you read the story to your class, or use a guest reader while you do the filming. Ask your videographer to zoom in from time to time on the illustrations or on the faces of the listening children in your audience. If you plan to include children in the video, your school may require you to have signed release forms from the parents. The video may be checked out and taken home or used within the classroom.

Create a PowerPoint presentation or video using children's illustrations of the figures or of the story scenes (use illustrations from last year's class or from a colleague's class) and either the children's words or yours. Scanning or filming student illustrations and then combining them with a written or spoken text give status to the drawings and the artists who created them. I once watched a Hungarian children's television program that used this idea. The figures and background drawings were standard kindergarten art; but when the camera zoomed in on them, or the storyteller moved them as she talked and her voice conveyed excitement in the story, the children were captivated. If you make a PowerPoint presentation, save it as a show on your desktop menu so that children can watch it without help during center time. By the way, if you use their drawings, give credit to all the artists at the end of the presentation so that they can see their names appear. Use the slowest speed of the animation that scrolls their names up the screen.

Investigate the availability of videos or DVDs that are factually correct. In their desire to be entertaining, some producers of Bible story videos have included incidents that have no biblical basis but yet are woven in with the biblical account as if they were part of it. Should truth be taking a backseat to artistic license when it comes to God's Word? Preview videos for accuracy before you hit the play button and view it with young children.

If you decide to tape an educational TV show, be aware of copyright restrictions that apply, and act honorably. If you love a particular program, it fits perfectly with your curriculum, and you know you will want to use it year after year, either buy a copy or check with the producers to ascertain whether or not you can have permission to use the tape until it wears out. PBS, for example, has generous (but not unlimited) rights for educators. Check their website for details.

Tony Stead (2002), in his book on teaching children to write nonfiction, suggests stopping a video several times during the program and having children retell what they have learned at that point rather than viewing the entire program first. If you decide to do this, when you preview the video, note natural stopping places. If you feel this will ruin the enjoyment of the viewing experience, watch it all the way through the first time, and then the next day, watch it again doing the stopping and retelling.

Exploration of an Internet site designed specifically for children— think of it as an information text—usually requires help from an adult (a parent volunteer, a librarian, an aide) or an older child. When you search for websites appropriate for children, also check class sites or school sites. These often have reports of class units with pictures, writing, and so on. There are more sites targeted for elementary children than for preschool children, but your adult helper can "translate" material to the children's level if necessary. Some sites may be useful for pictures even if the site is aimed at older children and adults. Keep the following suggestions in mind if you hope to keep your helpers long-term:

- Don't put your helpers in front of a computer with students without giving specific directions.

- Do your own search to determine what websites will provide the input you want, and make sure the sites are still valid.

- "Bookmark" those addresses or add them to your "favorites" list.

- Know what is on each site. Consider supplying a graphic organizer to guide exploration.

- Before enlisting helpers, try doing the task yourself under the same conditions—same directions, same number of students, same amount of time, similar distractions—to make sure it is doable.

4

Experts and Field Trips

When you decide to hand over input to someone else, particularly someone relatively unknown, you're taking a chance. There's no doubt about it: being a special speaker in a preschool classroom is tough. Anyone who knows how to relate well to young children is a jewel of great price. You can help potential speakers and yourself by discussing with them beforehand your general goals for their visit or the unit of study. (For example, say to your speaker, "I want my students to have a sense of what it feels like to be a blind child. What activities could you do with them to help them understand this?") You may already have a specific goal, or you may be open to different suggestions from the speaker—ideas that are sometimes even better than your suggestions. The bottom line: know where you're headed and make sure the speaker is headed in the same direction.

My husband's motto is "Don't assume anything." Our science curriculum suggested a number of interesting activities about skeletons in our unit on the body. We made backbone models out of pasta, we tapped our bones, we examined donated X-rays, and we squeezed a rag doll and tried to make it stand and sit up. Then someone volunteered the information that a relative of one of my students taught student nurses and had access to a life-sized skeleton. It sounded like a match to me. She had a skeleton, she was a teacher, and she had had plenty of practice speaking with and relating to at least one young child. (No doubt you've already seen the potential problems. You're smarter than I was.) I talked with her over the phone—briefly. She was delighted that we were interested in the skeleton, and she told me that she would be pleased to show it to the children. Because I neglected to clarify sufficiently what learning I hoped would take place, we ended up with a recital of the correct names of the bones—a presentation appropriate for student nurses but not for a group of energetic kindergartners. The moral of the story: Have a clear purpose, discuss it ahead of time with the speaker, and don't assume anything—get feedback from the speaker. Make sure she understands how much time she will have, and if there are other considerations such as students with limited English, discuss them as well.

Whatever your visiting expert does—reads a book aloud, demonstrates and involves children in an art technique or in correct tooth brushing—you may want to preserve a record through videotaping the presentation (with the expert's permission). This way you can review it later, stopping to retell, as Stead (2002) suggests, without interrupting your guest.

When you take a field trip, you go to the experts to see and hear about new things. To help children remember the different parts of the field trip, adapt Stead's (2002) "stop the video and summarize" idea. During one field trip to the airport, I took pictures of the different parts of the building and the equipment that we saw. Later the class retold the "story" of their field trip by using the pictures to jog their memory, and the book we made became part of our class library. (Consider sending your guide a copy of the book along with your thank-you note.)

Videotaping parts of the trip is another way to review the trip afterward. If you don't have a video recorder available, a small tape recorder can act as a low-cost, low-tech memory aid. Either tape the guide's words or ask children to take turns quickly summarizing input ("What did she say?") after each stop on the tour. Ensure that your students will be comfortable with this by practicing it the day before with them. Obviously the summary has to be quick because you need to keep up with the group, you need to be free to move around, and you don't want to break up the continuity of the trip. Afterward—perhaps while you wait for the bus—pretend to be a TV reporter. With microphone in hand, ask leading questions of different students in order to fix the details in their memory. Well-done brochures (with a map and pictures) from the site can fill the gaps.

Observations and Experiences

Suppose you want children to learn about ants. You could use a book or video for input, but direct observations (as opposed to watching a video) and hands-on experiences (when appropriate) satisfy the desire of preschoolers to get up close and be physically involved in learning. In the following example, observation was the primary means of input, but books and cassette tapes played a supporting role.

This example takes us back to the science fair. The project that year involved ants—not just run-of-the-mill ants, but giant one-inch-long ants, whose mature eggs are five-eighths of an inch long and look like white Good & Plenty candies. A parent helped us build an ant farm; we filled it with dirt and dropped the ants into their new home. Students experimented by dropping bits of different foods in to find out what the ants ate. The ants ignored potato chips and cookie crumbs, but they stopped and licked sugar; and though they seemed to prefer live protein, they usually had to make do with recently swatted flies.

The children observed the ants every day for three weeks. During that time I read books about ants to the children, and they listened to a tape I made of unusual information about ants; I had gleaned the facts from the encyclopedia. After receiving this input, the children began using such words as *thorax* and *antennae*, and they studied the ants more carefully. I sat nearby and recorded their comments as they watched. Later I asked for group input. The following excerpts—a mixture of large- and small-group comments blended together—are from our final document, which was on display at the science fair along with the ants and the children's individual notebooks. Some of the children's observations are interpreted in terms of kindergarten experience, such as their expression "cooking the worm" (and yes, in case you've never listened closely to ants, they do make a sound when they're excited):

Our Journal of Learning About Ants
(Group Retelling) March/April 1991

March 11

We made a house for the big ants. We made it with wood and glass and screws. We put dirt in the ant farm. We put the ants in the ant farm. Two

of them got buried and we took them out. We lost an egg under the dirt.
They still have one. They are carrying it so they don't lose it ...

March 12

The big ants are making tunnels. An egg was wiggling. They had a big
hole. The big ants were talking. There are eleven. Some were buried before.
Their legs and their bodies are furry. The ants ate a fly ...

March 19

The ant bit the worm's tail to stop him from wiggling. [Some of the girls
watched the worm and the ants for a while. These are their comments.]
They have nice tunnels where they cook and sleep. They're cooking the
worm. [Mrs. H. asks how.] With their mouth they cook it. They just bite
'em. That's where they cook it down there. There's an oven down here
where you can't see it [A student points toward the bottom of the ant
farm.] There are three ants trying to pick up the worm. They took him
to the very bottom. The worm is all by himself in the bottom ...

March 25

Dani commented that part of his legs is pointy.... The part close to his
body is a little fat. The back of his legs, closest to his body, is black, and
the front is a little black and orange ...

April 2

Mako says one ant jumped. He sees more eggs. He says there are nine.
They're like fingers held together, but small. Dani thinks one is licking the
egg. She wonders where the queen is. Ferdie says one is kissing his tail.

61

Dani reminds him that ants don't have tails. Abby says, "One is cleaning himself." Pablo sees the combs on their legs ...

April 3

Tina saw an ant carrying an egg in the tunnel. She thinks that maybe the ants are carrying the eggs to a safe place. Ferdie thinks that the ants are licking the eggs, but he doesn't know why they are doing it. Abby says that the ants think that the eggs are sweet like honey so they like to suck them.... One egg is separate from the bundle ...

Experiences such as food preparation and cooking can also be used for input. Making butter by shaking cream in a jar has a temporal structure to it—first it looked like this, then we did this, and then it looked like this—that both supports the learning of ordinal numbers and aids in recall of the process. This is an easy retelling experience with which to start. Keep a sample of the cream from the jar before it was shaken, of the butter in the jar, and of a buttered cracker to serve as prompts; tell the children to put the samples in order and then to describe how they made butter.

One of our class traditions at Thanksgiving each year was to make pumpkin pies for our "helpers" (bus driver, librarian, cleaning lady, gardener, principal). The input included the recipe (posted on chart paper and referred to as we cooked), and the actual cooking. We often sent a copy of the retold recipe to the school newspaper; however, baking a pumpkin pie by using the following retold recipe would *not* be a good idea:

How to Make Pumpkin Pie
From the Kindergarten Class

With the holidays coming, you might want to consider making a traditional treat. The kindergarten class suggests pumpkin pie and is happy to share this taste-tested recipe with you.

Get a pumpkin. Put sugar in a bowl. Put flour in the bowl and two cups of shortening. Stir it and mix it. You punch it down so it's flat. You put it in a muffin pan. Put it in the oven. Then you put pumpkin pie with the crust. You cut the pumpkin and take the seeds out and put it in a pan in the oven. When it's done you take it out of the oven and take the peel off and mash it. You put cinnamon and ginger and salt and yeast[1] and milk and sugar. You put the crust in the oven with the pumpkin pie and let it cook and cool and then you eat it. We are sure you will enjoy eating your pie. Ours was very good. It's fast to make too.

4

Each day's classroom experience offers input if as a closing activity the teacher asks the class members to comment on what they did that day. Keeping a written class journal from the first day on allows teachers and students to reflect on learning, both daily and over time, and can be used on a class web page or in newsletters to parents.

Consider adapting the idea of a math journal. Some math programs suggest giving math problems to children to solve so that they discover math principles using manipulatives in a "lab" situation. Afterward in their math journals they explain what they did and how it worked. Liping Ma (1999) describes a similar method of learning

---

[1] Some children think that you don't need the yeast, but others are adamantly sure that you do. It may be a matter of taste. You can decide whether you want to include it.

math in which Chinese children were encouraged to solve a problem in different ways and discuss strategies afterward so that they gained a better understanding of the mathematical principles involved. There are times when a kindergarten class might try to solve a mathematical problem or situation and then solidify their learning by describing or retelling it with words or pictures.

We did the problem-solving element of this idea after a child mentioned, during Bible class, that her parents put money in the offering at church. This caused a stir as most of the rest agreed that their parents also did this. We happened to be in the middle of a math unit on money—it couldn't have been more perfect. I told them that I knew how their parents figured out how much money to put in the offering. This fascinated them, and I explained tithing in terms of ten pennies and then ten dollars.

At the end of the money unit a few days later, I decided to create a small store and let them buy some cheap piñata-type toys. Suddenly it hit me that I could make this more interesting by including tithing. The next day I showed them the displayed toys (from a distance because I didn't want them to know yet that the toys were all marked nine cents), and I gave each child a dime. I told them that they could buy the toys. They were excitedly planning what they would buy when I reminded them that there was something they had to do before they spent their money. (Silence and puzzled looks followed.) "Something we *always* do first when we get money," I prompted.

"Oh, I know," said one. "We have to give one penny back to God first to say thank you."

All happily agreed. But then they realized they had a problem. Monetary value is abstract, and coins are concrete. How in the world do you get a penny when all you have is a dime?

I jingled a handful of pennies thoughtfully, then more loudly. No one caught on. The dimes were staring them in the face. Staring pointedly at pennies spread out on my palm, I said, "I could probably trade money with you if you need it."

Finally one mathematician asked tentatively, "Would you give me ten pennies for a dime?"

4

With the impasse broken, she traded, dropped a penny in the "offering bag," and bought her toy. Her classmates followed suit.

Unfortunately I was not alert enough at the time to realize that I could have had them retell how they did it. A group retelling of this could have been: "We wanted to buy toys at the store. Everybody had one dime. We had to give a penny of it back to God. We traded the dime for ten pennies. We gave one penny to God and bought toys with the nine pennies."

You may not think that you would do such math activities often enough to merit a journal, and perhaps you would rather have a space on the wall for math discoveries dictated as a group or as individuals. On the other hand, once you start doing a journal, you might surprise yourself.

CHAPTER 5

Output: Choices, Choices, Choices

Retelling has traditionally been associated with an individual response—either oral or written—to a story. We've already broadened input beyond a story; now we'll be doing the same with output. We're focusing on young children whose memory, thinking, and language skills are usually not as developed as those of older children. Yet, they can amaze us with their output and thinking, usually in a context of adult support, although peer contributions are valuable as well. An adult acts as a cheerleader, albeit a quiet one, by mirroring the facial expression of the teller, by murmuring "And then?" when a child seems to lose concentration, or by simply looking interested in what the child is saying. The teacher also encourages optimal recall and organization by mingling nonverbal and verbal retellings and by providing the scaffolding the children need to reach higher.

Age and developmental levels, however, are not the only reasons for including other means of retelling. We know that while spoken and written language are the most common means of communication, many ideas can be communicated through body language or visual arts. We speak of what a person's actions *tell* us or what a particular piece of art *says* to us. Sometimes these ways of communicating reveal understandings or misunderstandings that verbal language does not, so widening the means of retelling for young children makes sense.

In this chapter we'll look at when to use different types of retellings—group or individual, guided or unguided, verbal or nonverbal. In the next chapter, we'll look at more specific uses of them.

Group or Individual Retellings?

Group retellings are appropriate when children need support because of developmental factors, unfamiliarity with a task, or the difficulty of a task. Some young children lag behind their peers in language fluency and vocabulary. In a group retelling they experience minimal personal risk while enjoying involvement in the activity, and at the same time they are informally instructed by other children's input. Some children face a similar problem when they must listen to a language that is not their native one and respond in that language. Some children lack internalized aids to memory such as an understanding of story structure or extensive background knowledge, which act as advance organizers. Again, those who have developed in these areas carry the ball for those who have not.

Part of our job as teachers is to draw in the less-eager participants in the class through comments and questioning. Every class has children who take to retelling easily and who volunteer readily. It's easy to be so grateful for this that we overlook the opportunity to draw others in as well. Notice how an English language learner in the group is included in the following example:

Teacher   (She has already elicited from students the general body shape of the caterpillar.) What else can we tell others about our caterpillar? Daniel?

Daniel   Our caterpillar has orange stripes.

Teacher   (She allows processing time by speaking slowly and thoughtfully.) Daniel said, "Our caterpillar ... has ... orange stripes." (She uses her finger to trace a stripe pattern on the drawing while saying *stripes*.) Does everyone agree?

Nick   Except they're not on his head.

Daniel   Our caterpillar has orange stripes on his body.

Teacher   Is that better, everyone?

Karla   We could say the stripes go around his body because people might think they go up and down.

Teacher   Do you want to add that to your sentence, Daniel, or shall we make another sentence?

Daniel   Our caterpillar has orange stripes that go around his body.

Karla   Yeah.

Teacher   Daniel, would you like to color stripes on his body while I write your words? (Daniel colors orange stripes in the large outline drawing of the body of the caterpillar attached to the board in front of the group, while the teacher adds the sentence to those already on the board, saying the words as she writes them.)

5

Teacher	What about his head? (Teacher points to the head on the outline drawing.) Mi Heh, what color is his head? (Teacher again points to the head on the outline drawing.)
Mi Heh	Black and yellow.
Teacher	Yes, black and yellow. With stripes? (She makes a striping motion on the head of the drawing.)
Mi Heh	(She shakes head.) Like this. (She makes a dotting motion.)
Teacher	Is that right, class? (All agree.) What do we call them? Karla?
Karla	Spots and they're yellow. (All agree with this.)
Teacher	Yellow spots ... So, what shall I write about his head, Mi Heh?
Mi Heh	Head is black and yellow spots.
Karla	His head is black *with* yellow spots.
Teacher	Okay? (All agree.) Mi Heh, come and color his head black with yellow spots. (Teacher points to drawing and holds out markers.)

If a task is unfamiliar to the group as a whole, it is usually easier and more efficient to explain and model the process to the entire group rather than to individuals. Once the teacher has modeled the process, instead of requiring children to do it on their own immediately, she continues to model it while gradually decreasing her input and increasing that of the students. The next step is to ask whether there are those who would like to do the task themselves.

In addition to helping children become accustomed to focusing their attention and recalling material, a group retelling promotes a sense of group identity and support. A sense of "we" develops gradually through being involved in shared activities rather than through being placed in a group setting. This sense of mutual acceptance encourages children to participate in reaching common goals.

Individual retellings require more of a child in terms of attention, recall, and language. These retellings usually require the use of aides or volunteers or a bigger investment of time by the teacher. In return, individual retellings offer us a more comprehensive sense of what a child knows and the charm of individual expression, as seen in Bryon's story:

Daniel Says No
By Bryon

Ders a king an' he sent all his armies an' they wooked an' den some boys came an' they were kinna big. An' then they said, "Come an' eat at my table," and Danny, he had thwee friends and he said, "Uh oh," 'cause God doesn't want them to eat the food. An' they hadda learn da alphabet an' dey went over to one of da guys an' dey said, "Can't we have a little test?" An' he said, "Fo' ten days can you just give us begetables and water?" An' he said, "Okay, I can handle it fo' ten days." Dey keep on eating vegetables.

At some point we want children to become independent, responsible learners—to leave the safety of the group and to form habits of listening carefully, pulling information from memory, and expressing themselves clearly. Some children leap toward this goal, and their words spill out enthusiastically from their first retelling on. Others need encouragement and support of some kind as they do individual retellings. With time, they too will become comfortable and skilled.

Individual retellings are delightful additions to portfolios and displays. Both teachers and parents can assess a child's progress as they examine the child's work. When the retelling is one-on-one, the teacher has the opportunity to pinpoint areas of need and to interact more closely with each child than he would during a group retelling.

Guided or Unguided Retellings?

The amount of guidance that is needed or given to children varies according to a number of factors:

- The first involves background. Some children have heard the stories or information before; some haven't. There are homes in which limits on parental energy and time may push routine story reading aside. But in others, story reading is part of the daily ritual, and children like Jack in the following retelling are familiar with story language and structure:

Jesus and the Leper
By Jack

Der was a man dat lived with leprosy an' no one would get close to him, not even touch him. Not even his daddy an' mama. An' so one day he saw Jesus tryin' a make these other people better. And he said, "He can make me better. I'm going to go over there with the other people." And so he did. An' everybody said, "The man with leprosy, the man with leprosy, get over here! Come on!" And so they did, the people. He had all sores on him. He asked Jesus, "Can you make me better?" And He did. He went off an' said, "Jesus made me better. Jesus made me better, everyone!" Everybody said, "That's wild!" And that was the end.

- Second, facility with the language of instruction plays a major role in determining how much help children need in order to succeed in retelling. One year I didn't have the Christmas story flannelgraph figures available during our story time because another class was using them. Rather than change our schedule, I decided to tell the story without pictures. My English language learners were conversing in English reasonably well during class by that point in the year, so I assumed that they could manage without the figures. I was wrong. Being in control of language (when speaking) is quite different from being on the receiving end when another person controls the vocabulary, syntax, and speed of input. The quality of their retellings plummeted. They needed visual aids to support attention, understanding, and recall.

- Third, the time of the year and the amount of experience the class has had with retelling have an effect on children's facility with the language and make a great deal of difference in how

5

much support you need to provide them. Logically, we expect that children will mature during the course of a year and will need less help as time passes. We also know that external circumstances and stress affect all of us. As illustrated in my previous example, Christmas, with all its excitement and distractions, was not the best time to ask children to listen and retell in a second language without offering visual support to them.

- Fourth, the difficulty of the material affects how much guidance children require. We've already touched on the difference between using narrative and expository material and on elements that make material easier to recall and retell. This is not to imply that material that is not ideal for retelling must be discarded. However, if you choose to use something that is more difficult, you must be willing to guide children through their retelling of that material.

- Fifth, differences among children's abilities may prompt us to offer more hints and information to one child than to another.

- Sixth, our purpose dictates whether we correct mistakes or whether we supply missing information during the retelling. If we are comparing retellings, we want to hold the amount of guidance constant and correct mistakes later. If fluency and confidence are our goals, interrupting their train of thought with corrections acts as a brake with some children. Some refuse to keep going unless we give them the information they can't recall. Others, like Caleb, plow right on through any memory problems:

The Fiery Furnace
By Caleb

Meshach, Abednego, and I don't know the last one and then they went to another country where a king was. And then he built a big statue made outta gold and then he said, "When I play some music, you must bow down." And when the music played, Meshach and Abednego didn't bow down and I don't know the other's name. And then they had to go to the king and the king said, "I'll give you one more chance," and they said, "No thanks." And then they got tied up and thrown into the fire. And then they were walking around in the fire, and then the king opened the door of the fire. "Wait a minute, didn't we throw three people in there?" " 'Es we did, captain." And the king called out, "Meshach, Abednego, and I don't know," and they came out and talked to the king and the king said, "You must obey their God."

- Seventh, we're all familiar with the effects that late nights and family challenges have on children. As a teacher, you do your best, but there are times when—as demonstrated in the following story—no matter how much support you give, no matter how many prompts or hints you offer, it won't be enough, and you just accept that philosophically:

Jesus and the Leper
By Michael

He got healed. By Jesus.

As a general rule, when most children first begin retelling, they need more support because the task is unfamiliar. Reviewing unusual vocabulary before asking for a retelling, murmuring verbal prompts ("And then what happened?"), and making nonverbal helps available (pictures of the three or four main scenes of the story for the children to refer to if needed) facilitate retelling. Gradually their need for this support will decrease. If you are collecting stories for portfolios, include notes of how much support they needed individually (extensive verbal prompts, use of pictures, and so on) to help you gauge their progress.

Depending on what you hope to accomplish through retellings, you can provide further guidance to your students after a few retellings by talking with them about what makes a good retelling. If your immediate goal is to promote children's skill in retelling—to help the children sharpen it as a tool—then calling attention to it may be useful if you keep any instruction developmentally appropriate. Ask your students what makes a good retelling, and get responses from the older preschool children. Then make a short "prompt" chart to remind children what to listen for before they retell. Refer to the chart again before the retelling to remind children what to include in their retelling. If your goal is primarily volitional (wanting them to decide to treat others kindly or to obey their parents), affective (emphasizing love toward God and trust in Him), or general language fluency, stressing structure tends to detract from attaining the goal. You can also use a less-formal approach to motivate children to improve their retellings through the use of drama; this approach will be discussed later.

Deciding how much support to provide is a balancing act. We balance our desire for children to meet educational goals, our desire for them to grow in taking responsibility for their learning, and our desire for them to feel secure and to feel positive about themselves and learning.

Our personal backgrounds, personalities, cultures, beliefs, and experiences enter in as well. If we err, then it is wise in the long run to err on the side of providing more guidance rather than less in early education, particularly in the beginning.

Verbal or Nonverbal Retellings?

In early education, verbal and nonverbal means of output are often woven together into a rich and satisfying tapestry. Nonverbal retellings, such as murals and pantomime, stand on their own, but linking them to oral or written language activities extends their usefulness. Single pictures are usually limited in how much of a story they can convey. With young children they often act as the stimulus for a retelling. They're similar to phrases that need the rest of the sentence in order to express the thought completely. Most of the picture-related ideas in the chapters that follow are paired with verbal retellings. Most of the ideas that are primarily verbal include the use of pictures or other nonverbal materials as supports. These ideas are intended to stimulate your creativity. I've included simple ones that require very little in the way of tools, time, and technology, and others that are more elaborate. There's nothing wrong with a "plain vanilla" retelling, but sometimes you may feel in the mood for splurging on something different.

5

CHAPTER 6

Output: A Grab Bag of Ideas

During an individual retelling, an adult sets the task by asking the child to retell, provides an audience, prompts or asks for amplification if necessary, and on occasion records the child's words. During a group retelling, the teacher must also provide the social structure and guidance for a group of young children to work together. The next two chapters provide a grab bag of retelling ideas. This first section offers additional ideas and suggestions on recording verbal retellings. The rest of the ideas in this chapter focus on prompting recall and organizing it. Chapter 7 presents different approaches to retelling that are a mixture of the types introduced in chapter 5.

Recording Individual Retellings

Students may try to write their own version of a retelling if they have some knowledge of letters and sounds. I had them do this for very short student observations in science. The following is one entry in a student's ant observation journal:

Mach 14
the Ants MAD thAR tUNS And it is KloSR too the BadM.

See if you can guess the following story that one child decided to type on the computer during center time:

> ken sa waz anger at david pecas he was jaolis av david pecazdavid waslovedby popopecas hehad cioldgaliiththeind

Younger or less-advanced students may enjoy "writing" their story (scribbling in "cursive" or using random letters) and then retelling it. To preserve this so that others may enjoy it, record their retelling on audiotape or videotape or write their words below their writing.

Obviously you can record retellings by hand-writing them, but unless you know shorthand or you know that the retellings will be very short, try to find some other way. Scribbling furiously, trying to keep up with a child's speech, doesn't always result in a perfect transcription and, as you can imagine, is both tiring and time consuming. Instead, you might secure the help of a fast-typing aide or parent who can act as the students' scribe in the writing or computer center for a day or two a week. I did most of the typing myself during center time and found that each child took an average of three to four minutes to retell the stories I've used as examples.

If absolute accuracy is important to you (if you're doing a study, for example) or if the typist is extremely slow, tape the child speaking *as you type*. If you tape first and leave all the typing until later, children tend to speak more rapidly resulting in more difficult transcription. Even if you miss part of what they say while you're typing and you have to fill in the holes later by listening to the tape, you still are ahead and haven't had to keep asking the children to wait or to repeat themselves.

6

Consider creating a class recording studio center. If possible, take your class to visit a real one so that they can see how a studio is set up and what the different roles are in the studio. Teach children how to use the tape recorder to record their retelling. Post picture directions on the wall beside the recorder. It also helps to put labels on the recorder. Our recorder had a piece of red electrical tape on the stop button, a green piece on the forward button, and a yellow piece on the record button. Using a handheld microphone or one on a stand rather than the built-in microphone on the recorder is a nice touch. Enclose the area with curtains or dividers to set it apart and hopefully reduce some of the outside noise. Create a warning light with a colored bulb and a shadeless lamp (or a simple fixture and bulb mounted on a board) outside the enclosed area that children can switch on to request a quieter recording environment.

Provide variety by videotaping a class retelling or an individual retelling by using a traditional video camera, a digital camera in its video setting, a digital video camera, or a webcam. If you don't own any of these, if your classroom has a dinosaur of a computer, or if the thought of technology makes you nervous (just the vocabulary can be intimidating, let alone all the programs and possibilities), perhaps one of your parents or someone else in the community has the equipment and expertise to come in once or twice a semester to record children's retellings while you work with the rest of the class. The possibilities are intriguing. Here are a few to get you started:

- Capture a retelling by a child who may or may not be using pictures as prompts.

- Capture a retelling by a child who is using flannelgraph figures or a wordless book.

- Capture a retelling session between a shy child (or one with language difficulties) and a puppet or a session that shows a child teaching the story to a circle of doll students.

- Film a group drama retelling.

- Take still pictures of a child's retelling and her illustrations, and make a digital book by combining them with the typed text of the retelling through use of a program such as Movie Maker (for Windows), iMovie (for Mac), Kid Pix, or PowerPoint (Skouge 2004).

- For an individual retelling or a group retelling, use an art program such as Kid Pix, which will allow children to use a computer to draw their illustrations.

For more ideas involving technology, particularly for children with disabilities or language challenges, read the delightful recounting by James R. Skouge (2004) about his use of technology to preserve the culture of the Pacific islands and his pointers on teaching children to use it. Much of this technology was not available to me when I taught, but I followed his directions to make a digital big book for my granddaughter, using photos her mother had taken of her. I can assure you that it is relatively easy to do. It occurred to me that using a webcam to videotape a child's retelling should also work and, sure enough, it did. Expand the borders of your experience bit by bit; we ask children to do it, so why shouldn't we? Even if you have a parent or another volunteer come in to do the recording, you need ideas to plan such activities. The audiovisual output would be a delightful addition to any child's portfolio. Another possibility is to suggest that parents who have the technology make a recording at home and bring it in for the child to share with the class.[1]

82

I've mentioned our science fair project involving giant ants, a subject we covered for several years. One year I decided that the children would make a videotape of what they'd learned. Then when parents came to the fair they could watch their child chattering away about various related ant topics, such as ant eggs and the different snacks we tried to feed the ants. Each child chose a topic to talk about, and a parent offered to come in and videotape it. I made one mistake though—we practiced first. When they redid the retelling for taping, all the sparkling enthusiasm and detail of the first telling was lost. After all, they seemed to reason, we already did this once. I should have gotten both on tape. You live and learn.

Recall and Organization

Memory Games

We've already noted that recalling expository material is more difficult than recalling a story and that group retellings facilitate the task. If you've ever played a version of the children's game "Going to Grandma's"—with its cumulative lists that are created as participants respond to the statement "I went to Grandma's (or to camp or to kindergarten) and I took ..."—then you know that it isn't easy to recall random lists of information. You can use a modified format of this memory game anytime, but it is particularly helpful if the input you want children to recall is not well-structured and you want to separate the steps of recall and organization from retelling. It's also a

[1] A video file tends to be fairly large (approximately 23 MB for a three-minute story that becomes 8 MB when saved in Windows Movie Maker) so you will probably want to save children's retellings to a flash drive or a rewritable CD rather than keeping them on a computer hard drive. Saving them this way also makes it possible to add them to individual student portfolios.

helpful activity to use if a large number of your students are learning English as a foreign language, and they need the repetition.

To make the memory task easier and more fun for young children, use picture prompts (draw or photocopy pictures from the book or other material you're wanting the children to remember) or word prompts if the children have some knowledge of letters and sounds. Make sure that you have blank cards available in case someone remembers a point that wasn't illustrated.

In case you missed playing this game during your childhood, it helps to have children sitting in a circle. The first person completes the sentence. The next person must repeat the first person's contribution before adding his own. The third person must give the first and second persons' words before adding hers, and so it continues around the circle. Suppose the class has listened to a book about turtles. The beginning of the recall session might sound something like the following:

Keve: Turtles have a hard shell. [Keve receives a picture of a turtle shell from the teacher, shows it to everyone, and then places it facedown on the floor in front of him.]

Eva: Turtles have a hard shell and they like to eat lettuce. [Eva receives the picture from the teacher, shows everyone the picture of a turtle nibbling on vegetables, and places the picture facedown on the floor in front of her.]

Dominick: Turtles have … umm, what was the first one? [Looks at Keve, who shows his card again and returns it facedown.] They have a hard shell and they eat lettuce and … they like carrots too. [Shows the card he

84

shares with Eva because it has both lettuce and carrots on it. Otherwise, Dominick or the teacher draws a picture of a carrot on a blank card.]

Before you read a particular book to your students the first time or before you review it, it's a good idea to tell children that they will be playing a game of remembering the information. (This is the preschool version of warning them that "it will be on the test.") Decrease the difficulty of the activity by forming teams, leaving the cards faceup, or allowing the children to choose their cards before the game starts. Adding organizational categories also helps some children recall what they heard. On the board, draw pictures of the following: a mouth representing food, a square representing descriptive features, and a house representing habitat. Explain that we all know, of course, that a turtle doesn't have a mouth like ours, but the picture on the board is to help the children remember that part of the book described what a turtle eats. The square is to make them think of a photograph in the book that showed what a turtle looks like. The house is to remind them what the book said about where turtles live.

On another day before you do the actual retelling, you may choose to organize the mass of details that children have recalled. Spread out the pictures and ask children to stand next to theirs. Instruct the ones whose pictures are about the food a turtle eats to take their picture and sit in the large circle marked on the floor. Do the same with the other categories, sending each group to some specific place (maybe the large triangle on the floor, the red table, the green rug). If you want them to discuss the order of their observations within the group first, give them a short time to organize themselves; then begin the group retelling, group by group. Not only is the movement enjoyable, the physical reorganization reinforces the idea of separate categories.

6

Some older preschoolers like the challenge of doing this activity without prompts, especially if you express amazement that they can even *consider* doing it without the pictures. (You may say, "At first I thought to myself, *maybe* they can retell the book *without* the pictures, but then I thought, no, I don't think they can remember all those things." At this point at least one person is sure to protest, "Yes, we can." You respond, "Really? You can remember all those things?" The movement has gathered strength at this point, and several affirm that they can. A few cautious souls may qualify their involvement by saying that they can remember *most* of it.) Let them try with the understanding that they can look at the cards at any time if they need them. When they're done, express great admiration for all that they have remembered. Ask if they want to check the cards to see if there is anything else they want to add.

Graphic Organizers

We've already touched on using graphic organizers with information books to prepare the way for input by creating listening expectations. If you've approached a book that way, all you have to do at the end is to ask children to supply the information in each category and you're ready to retell. You can do this as a group or individually—depending on your students' maturity and ability—using letters, words, or pictures.

In *Tell Me a Story*, elementary school reading teacher Jill Hansen (2004) suggests using graphic organizers with retelling. She includes reproducible blackline masters in the back of the book; however, you can draw your own or download some from the Internet (see appendix). My favorites from her book are those emphasizing sequence and one that resembles a kindergarten drawing of the sun. Because the book focuses on children in the primary grades, Hansen suggests having each child first draw small pictures to show story sequence and then label them using at least a beginning letter or two if a descriptive word or phrase is too difficult. (A picture of Joseph telling his dream to his brothers might be labeled "J d b" for Joseph, dream, brothers.) Some kindergartners can complete this task on their own. To provide more guidance for younger children, decide as a class what the major scenes will be and come up with the descriptive labels for each space or box of the organizer. Using this input, create a master with labels that you can photocopy so that students only need to draw the pictures.

If doing several pictures is too demanding for your students to do individually, turn the activity into a small-group project. Again, decide as a class on the four or five scenes of the story and how to label them. This time though, instead of having the entire organizer (with very small pictures) on one page, use a different blank page for each box. For the story of Jairus' daughter, you might have scenes depicted as follows: "The little girl was sick. Her father went to Jesus. A man said the little girl was dead. Jesus made the little girl alive. The little girl ate some food." (If you let the class write the descriptors, you might have something like "LTL GRL SK" for the first page, "H F W T JS" for the second, and so on.) Schedule a short break between the class discussion and the creation of the masters so that you can photocopy enough sets for the class. According to the number of scenes, divide the class into several small groups so that each person in a group draws a different sequence picture. The easiest way to decide who does which picture in a group project is to place the sheets with the descriptions facedown on the table and let each child choose one. If you want to integrate some math instead, count around the table or draw numbers.

6

Having an organizer with physically defined empty spaces on it that need to be filled appeals to some children. Suppose you choose to enlarge a sequential graphic organizer that resembles movie or filmstrip frames. Filling each frame with a blank sheet of paper allows you to write the class' descriptors of each scene on the page. The pages are then taken out and duplicated if you want the picture and descriptor to appear on the same page. If there are only a few scenes, then this may need to be a small-group project; however, usually the class can recall enough scenes to make it a class project. If you have students who are perfectionists and are never satisfied with their first drawing attempt, consider putting the descriptor on one frame and the picture on the next. (Remember seeing some of the earliest movies, before the actors actually spoke? There were frames that showed a sentence describing the action that was coming, and then there were frames of action.) Don't forget to add a title frame at the beginning and a credits frame at the end. Put the organizer on the wall as a display or attach the ends to dowels to make a scroll that you can roll through a frame to give the appearance of a TV screen. Sequential organizers for stories may act as an outline for a more complete retelling by the group or by individuals, or they may be the final retelling.

Hansen (2004) suggests rereading the story afterward to verify that everything has been remembered. Adding this step also serves as a check on the correctness of the material. Your aim in doing the retelling will dictate whether or not you want to do this with young children. Given young children's attention spans, you might want to do this on the second day, reminding children to keep their eyes on their version as you read or tell the story. Have they forgotten anything? Once students are familiar with the activity, you can add some variety. Instead of rereading the story, place in your listening center a taped version of your original telling, along with the

6

filled-in graphic organizer or pictures, and ask the children to check independently for missing information. If they find something missing in a group retelling, praise them for good listening and thinking, and share their ideas with the group.

Vary the use of graphic organizers by occasionally providing an organizer that has been filled in with all but one of the scenes. (In the beginning, choose a main scene, such as Daniel with the lions, a scene that the children would enjoy doing. Later you might choose one that emphasizes a less-favorite but important part of the story, such as Daniel praying at his window.) Instruct the children to draw the scene that is missing. Let them use their organizer as they retell the story orally to a classmate, an older student, a puppet, you, or their parents.

Hidden Pictures

Do you remember having an Advent calendar when you were small? Even if you were disappointed with the pictures, there was still an element of anticipation involved, wasn't there? One way to emphasize story structure and guide retellings is to create a hidden picture display—a very distant relative of the Advent calendar.

To introduce the idea, use a large sheet of heavy poster board and make three or four large flaps in a row, with each being large enough to hide a picture behind. Place the main scenes from the story in sequence behind these flaps. (If you don't have pictures and aren't an artist, make these by photocopying flannelgraph figures laid out in scenes or by drawing stick figure representations of the scenes.) The same effect can be achieved by hiding the pictures in large envelopes or folders labeled 1 through 4.

Another possibility is to make a reverse version of a one-line, giant pocket chart. Remember the early cardboard pocket charts that had small "pockets" that held the cards so that everything on them had to be above the pockets to be visible? In this situation, since you want almost everything to be hidden except for a small part at the top, make the pockets deep so that they'll reveal only a small portion of the pictures.

Tell the story, showing the appropriate picture at each point and then covering it up again. Children experience a sense of expectancy once they realize what is happening. Afterward, ask the children if they remember what happened first: Which picture is behind the first flap or hidden in the first pocket? Then what happened? Lift the flaps or take the pictures out to check. Can someone retell the story by using the pictures or by keeping them hidden? Did the student remember everything? Take a look at the pictures to check.

Once children are comfortable with the concept of major scenes, modify your use of pictures—maybe tell the story without the picture scenes. Afterward, mention that you didn't have pictures. If there had been pictures, what scenes would they have shown? Draw them yourself as the children suggest them, or once the class has decided which scenes are necessary, ask those who suggested the scenes to draw them. After putting the pictures in place, ask for volunteers to retell the story using them.

Instead of discussing the pictures first as a group, a more challenging modification after the class has heard the story would be to ask a handpicked group of three or four to create the pictures for the story without letting anyone else in the class, including you, know what the scenes are. (Make sure the story that you use for this modification has a simple, clear structure and about four main scenes.) Have fun brainstorming, as a class, what the small group's picture choices might be before the group unveils the pictures. Let the group retell the story with the pictures in place. Did the class guess what the pictures were? After this initial example, let other groups do the same thing. You could choose to have all groups do the same story or take turns, each with a new story, over several weeks. The key to success is strong story structure and an accepting spirit on your part if their scenes don't match your chosen four. As long as they can retell the story using their pictures, great!

Mystery Pictures

When reviewing several stories at the end of a unit, my favorite activity involves mystery pictures. Here are the suggested steps:

- Tell the children that they are going to make "mystery pictures."

- They are to choose one story from a list of stories they've heard recently. I like to have at least four or five in the list.

- They are to draw a picture of part of that story, but *they are not to tell anyone* which story they picked (thus making them possessors of secret knowledge and power).

- Then you will come around and see if you can guess by looking at their picture which story they picked—it's their secret from you.

How good a guesser is the teacher? Her success depends to a large degree on how good the pictures are. What makes the activity so enjoyable for both children and the teacher is the teacher's ability to play a role, drawing attention to details of the drawing as she studies the picture and thinks aloud, possibly pretending to be more puzzled than she is so that the children are the ones in the know as long as possible. Give the children a few minutes and then begin

6

circulating, making such comments as, "Hmm, I see the sun … it looks like your story happened outside, at least part of it. I'll have to think hard about stories that happened outside. You keep working on your picture and I'll come back in a bit." Or you might say, "Well, two people standing with their hands stretched out to the side—I'm going to have to think about that one. Which story had two people standing like that? I'll come back in a bit when you've added more to your picture to help me figure it out." (If the picture is really stripped down and the child looks clueless about adding to it, I make a point of commenting on the background or other parts of their neighbors' pictures to give them ideas.)

Even if you can tell in the beginning what story is depicted by the drawing, try to stretch out the mystery: "Water, lots of water. I *think* I know which story you're drawing, but I'm going to let you do a bit more to make sure I'm right." When you actually guess, model your thinking aloud to draw their attention to what was important and helpful so that they will be more likely to repeat the process of giving attention to particular details in future drawings.

Kindergartners adore this activity. Knowing something that the teacher doesn't is so exciting for them! Now that you have the picture to act as a prompt for retelling, they can retell the story to the class, they can bestow the honor on a friend, or the class can retell it as a group. These pictures also make great displays for parents and other classes. Title them "Can You Guess the Story?" and either immediately provide a key (covered or upside down) or let the suspense build and provide the key a day or two later.

I used this activity with mystery pictures exclusively with narratives, but it could be used with expository material as well. Remember the examples in chapter 2 of group retellings about insects? At the end of our unit, I could have asked students to pick a bug and draw it without telling anyone which one it was. Or, with the ants, they could have illustrated their favorite detail of ant life and behavior. You guess what each picture is (maybe whisper your guess in that particular artist's ear so that the class can guess later). Once the picture is identified, the artist or the class as a whole retells what is known about the bug, or the artist expounds on his favorite observations or a particular part of the project.

Promoting Thinking Skills

When you review stories, add some thinking skills to the mix by putting figures from more than one story on the board at the same time. Or better yet, manage to drop the pile of figures from two stories such as David caring for his sheep and David and Goliath (having the figures mixed up before you drop them, but only you know that) so that they are out of order on the floor. Obviously you'll need help to separate these back into the correct stories. To do so, use two large circle outlines (made of hoops or yarn so that the circles can be moved) on the flannelboard or on the floor to sort the figures into two sets. Ask for the students' help in placing the figures in the correct circles based on the stories—a simple task.

The most interesting part of the activity involves the figures that are in both stories. How can the students show that? Let them brainstorm solutions. Tearing the figure in half isn't an option. The most common solution that I've heard is to lay the figure crosswise so that it touches both circles. You may want to accept that. You might purposely place the two circles so far apart that a child has to move them closer together to accomplish this. You might suggest that they move the circles even closer until they overlap, or you might "make a mistake" yourself while moving them so that they overlap briefly. Some children see the solution of overlapping circles, especially if you've already done something similar in math. You may offer the solution; it's up to you. Personally I like to make them puzzle a bit. If they don't see that overlapping the circles could solve their problem, their other solutions may be just as interesting. Where is the retelling in this? Retell the stories after everything is sorted or perhaps later if the students are caught up in the problem for a while.

Another activity has children finding the figures that don't belong. Add extra, unrelated figures when you put all the figures from one story on the board. If, for example, your story is the Christmas story, make a big production of thinking aloud as you pull the necessary figures out of a box. Include, for example, an elephant, a tent, a river, and Goliath with the normal ones. As you put the figures up on the board, you might say, "An elephant, yes, I'll need an elephant for the story, won't I?" Repeat "Won't I?" or say, "An elephant, right?" with a more questioning tone in your voice if they don't catch on the first time. They love to show their superior knowledge! Or just put all the figures on the board in the beginning and ask them what story they think you're going to review. Make sure that the number of unnecessary ones is small in the beginning so that the unrelated ones are obvious (a pair of elephants from Noah and the Ark placed with all the Nativity scene figures). You always have someone who points out that you have some pictures that don't belong. ("I do? Really? Which ones? Are you sure I won't need them?") Gradually increasing the ones that don't belong makes this activity more challenging.

CHAPTER 7

The Many Faces of Retelling

Labeled Pictures in Sequence

When a child draws a picture of part of the story after hearing it, very often either the child will label it with a few letters or words or the teacher will write the child's title or description of the scene. Most stories have one or two salient parts that children choose. Daniel is invariably in with the lions; few children will draw him praying at his window. In the story of Noah, you are more likely to see one of three scenes: the ark on the water, a picture with the rainbow, or the animals entering the ark. How can we build on these pieces of the story?

Perhaps the next day, after all the pictures are finished and on display in no particular order, the teacher can call attention to the sequence of the pictures:

- "Can we put these pictures in the order in which they happened in the story? Did God send the rainbow first, or did the animals go into the ark first?" Guide the group in sorting the pictures and putting them in left-to-right order. Naturally you'll have several pictures of one scene and perhaps pictures of more than one. How would you like to show that grouping? Form clusters going from left to right with space between each group? Display pictures of the same scene in vertical lines with space between each line? Group similar pictures under the first one so that a clear horizontal line is created? Using the example of Noah, you might have two pictures of the animals entering the ark, three pictures of the ark on the water, and nine rainbow pictures.

- "Are there any other parts of the story for which we don't have pictures? What are they?" Perhaps you ask for volunteers to draw the extra pictures. Perhaps you quickly draw a few simple pictures. (If you're artistic, this could be intimidating to your students if they compare their pictures with yours. I never had that problem!)

- Rather than using more pictures, you may ask for words to bridge the gap between pictures. In this example, when students are challenged to explain why there are animals and a big boat in the first pictures, students may volunteer to begin with a sentence similar to "God told Noah to build an ark because all the people were doing bad things." Between the first and second pictures the students may feel that they need to say something about God's closing of the door and the rain starting. How does the story move from the group of second pictures to the third? They know.

- If you write words and post them between the pictures, you read the words upon reviewing the story and ask volunteers to tell the part of the story that is illustrated. After a try or two, someone is sure to say, "I can do it all by myself." The reading then becomes telling. If there are additional parts of the story that you want to emphasize, include those after a few retellings.

Vary this format occasionally by using a color photocopier or scanner and printer to make overhead projector transparencies of children's drawings once they have been sorted. Students love to help pick representatives of the scenes to form a sequence. Shrink the pictures on your photocopier first if you want the scenes in order on a single transparency. Keep the transparencies to use another year as input.

Scanning the pictures and importing them into computer software such as PowerPoint or Movie Maker also allows individuals or groups of students to participate in creating sequences. The simplest way to do this is to file the scanned pictures in separate, numbered folders by scenes so that students open each folder (with or without your help), choose a picture for each scene from those available, and import the picture in the correct order. If your sequences are group projects, you can make sure that all the pictures are used if you move each picture out of the folder from which children choose and into another after it has been chosen by a group. If you still have too many of one scene, create a title page and a credits page to use two more as backgrounds. Depending on whether or not you have a projector available, have students use the sequences to retell the story in small groups or together as a class.

Occasionally, rather than using a linear left-to-right format, create a maze either on one page that students will do as a worksheet or on a giant-sized paper to hang on the wall for children to finger trace as they retell the story to the class. The maze should have four open areas for the four major scenes to be pasted in order as children reach that part of the maze. If the cutting and pasting of scenes would make the task too difficult for your children, design the maze with the pictures in place so that children go to the first picture first, then the second, and so on. Shrink the children's drawings to fit the open areas

7

if necessary. Afterward use the worksheet maze to prompt retellings. Use of a maze is a nice crutch for young children when they begin retelling. There is still some challenge involved since they have to order the pictures correctly when they retell, but they can usually come up with a sentence or phrase for each picture.

Murals and Picture Sequences

Murals are wonderful for emphasizing sequence and for giving children practice in working together. Young children need a teacher's help to review the sequence of the story, divide the story into enough "scenes" so that everyone in the class or small group has one, and model ways to equally distribute the scenes on the mural paper. There are never enough favorite scenes for everyone; that's a fact of life. Emphasize attractive parts of less-interesting scenes to help children see the artistic possibilities. Create word pictures that have children begging for every scene. Later have the children review the story verbally, and perhaps ask them to dictate a written version using the mural as a guide.

I like having the children use thick, brightly colored chalk sticks for murals. The chalk covers a large space quickly, and it doesn't break as easily as the thinner chalk. Having the students draw on a long sheet of paper taped to the chalkboard worked better than laying the strip on the floor or on a long table, because they were less likely to rest their hand on their neighbor's picture as they bent over their drawing. Roll up the mural to transport it to where it will be displayed and hang it high enough so that no one can rub up against it.

Using pictures from a commercially produced coloring book—the type that has several pictures for one story—is a variation of this. Photocopy the pictures so that there is a blank side for each, and then turn the pages blank side up and have each child pick a page. The class sequences the pictures, and the students retell the part of the story depicted on their individual page. For variety, I recorded this group retelling so that I could transcribe it and attach each child's contribution to that child's individual page. (The cassette later became part of the listening corner tape collection.) The pictures were taped together to create one long display.

Again, I used this activity for stories, but there is no reason why it couldn't be used for expository material. Suppose that during a math unit on shapes you had read books on shapes, done various activities with shapes, and taken a walk around the school looking for shapes. You can use a mural to retell your discovery of different shapes in your environment. For older preschoolers, you might organize your discoveries in a map format that retraces your walk and either draw pictures of the triangles, squares, circles, and rectangles you found in different places or use digital photos of them. If you aren't up to simple maps, the left-to-right progression of a mural still records the sequence. Consider using this format to retell what you saw on a field trip to the fire station, airport, or hospital.

7

Puppets and Visitors

Puppets with a personality, or even primed visitors, who draw the story sequence from children or who guide organized recall are fun for everyone. As we all know, children blossom in the role of the authority figure, the one who knows the right answers. Create a game-like atmosphere by having the puppet first sort the children's pictures and then tell the story out of order. Your students will be roaring with laughter and telling the puppet, "No, that's not the way the story went. *We'll* tell you the story!"

Another possibility is for the puppet to sort the students' pictures correctly but then tell the story using only the pictures so that much of the story is missing. Also, the puppet could claim to know the story and then make mistakes (the first time or two that you do this, a mistake should be dramatically preceded by a pause or a change in tone to cue students that something is wrong). The puppet can then benefit from the enthusiastic correction by the class. If students don't catch the mistake, the teacher may laugh and tell the puppet it made a few mistakes and then ask the students, "Can you help the puppet retell the story correctly?" If they can't, the teacher may have to review what the puppet said, hinting at the error through a change of tone or words or through a quizzical look at students at the appropriate time. This works best with older preschoolers who know the story well enough to be amused rather than confused by the puppet's mistakes.

Story character puppets of all kinds—finger puppets, stick puppets (which can also be used as action figures in a sandbox), sock puppets, simple marionettes, hand puppets—are perennial favorites with children. Some children are able to retell the story and move a puppet at the same time. Some concentrate so completely on either retelling the story or moving the puppet that splitting the storytelling and puppet moving makes more sense. If, for example, you take advantage of children's love of making hand shadows in a projector's light on the wall and you create stick puppets of the story characters and allow the children to move the puppets in the light, the children will probably be so caught up in the shadows they are creating that the story will suffer. You have several story text options:

- Reread the story.

- Record the reading or rereading and give children control over the tape recorder.

- Have other children retell or describe the actions of the puppets.

- Record a child's earlier retelling and give children control over the tape recorder.

- Type a child's retelling and read it or record yourself reading it.

If you record your reading or the children's retellings, the puppets could also be used during center time. Once the children realize that the more complex the story, the longer they can use the puppets, they tend to expand their retellings.

Books—Wordless, Coloring, Interactive, and Big

Think of the many types of books available for children. You can modify the variables of text, illustration, and presentation to experiment with something beyond the traditional storybook format of retelling.

7

Chart 1

Text: Who supplies it?	Illustrations: How are they created?	Presentation: What does it look like?
• Individual child • Group of children • Adult (commercial, puppet, teacher) • No text	• Drawn by children • Chosen by children • Provided (commercial, teacher drawn) • Created by children (using various art techniques, e.g., sponge painting, spatter painting, collage, craft foam, colored paper shapes) • Photographs (with children as actors, figures of clay or paper, action figures, puppets)	• Variations of size and shape • Paper, traditionally bound • Cloth or felt pages • Overhead transparency book tied together • Scroll • Circular story wheel • Computer book • Interactive book with movable figures • Audiobook

Wordless books and coloring books that are group created are similar to murals in that children need adult guidance in setting the scenes and in distributing them. However, the side-by-side-scenes format of a mural depicts so much in a large scale that the details become less important, and the discrete-scenes format of a book with limited or no text requires more detail. You can show your class other wordless books or coloring books as examples, pointing out the artist's details that make the picture more complete and interesting. Children don't want a coloring book with page after page of standard stick figures that are dead center and that have legs at parade rest and arms stretched out horizontally, do they? Brainstorm possible types of details that they could include. What are the characters in your scene standing on? Are they inside or outside—what could be drawn to show that? What type of clothes are they probably wearing? Later, as you circulate while children are drawing, ask individuals what they are thinking of adding to their picture to give it background and comment on the details you see to give others ideas of things to include in theirs. If someone is stuck, suggest that she ask a friend to help her think of appropriate details to add. Some may need help in fleshing out a stick figure so that there is something to color.

If these are group wordless books and you have a color photocopier or a scanner and color printer, consider occasionally making copies with them because the books look so professional when printed. To save ink, reduce the size of the pictures first or start with smaller pieces of paper and fine-point markers so that you can fit four pictures onto one sheet of paper.

We've already mentioned using PowerPoint and Movie Maker programs with scanned student artwork from previous years as input and creating picture sequences during output. Doing a different one each year builds your file of teaching materials and allows students the joy of sharing with the next year's class. Plan the pictures as you would for a wordless book or mural (rather than relying on whatever pictures the children decide to draw), scan the finished products, and enlist the children's help in arranging them in order using the slide sorter or storyboard options. Whether you create a wordless book, add narration by students, type their short description of their picture on the slide, or narrate it yourself is up to you. Another amusing use of scanned student pictures of one story would be to put them all in one file and set your computer's screensaver to run through them. The random generation of these would give everyone a laugh if they try to retell the story using them.

If the project is to make a photocopied coloring book of the story, it is easiest to give children each a yellow marker (with no other colors nearby) to draw their pictures. Encourage them to add background and details. Once they are done, go over the outlines with a black marker. Make only slight corrections as needed (such as tracing on the inside or outside of a line or closing off a space) so that children can still recognize their picture as theirs by more than their signature in the corner. If necessary, encourage them again to add details.

The authors of "The Power of Story Retelling" (Gibson, Gold, and Sgouros 2003) suggest having children make interactive storybooks. Each page of the storybook is a setting or scene. Figures of the characters are separate pieces that children manipulate as they turn the pages and retell the story. Your immediate reaction may be to imagine the chaos as children lose character pieces on the floor and in the trash can, followed by ownership arguments with a neighbor over the remaining figures. Since these authors know what young children are like, they suggest punching a hole near the top of each figure, tying a long piece of string or yarn to it, and then attaching the other end of all the strings to the cover of the book to resemble ribbon bookmarks. I would also add a pocket for each figure on the inside of the front cover to lessen the possibility of ripping dangling figures off the strings during storage.

Again, because elaborate backgrounds are rarely part of young children's pictures, provide an example the first time you create an interactive storybook as a class. Consider drawing and photocopying your scenes and figures for the children to color. Staple or bind the scenes in order and help children "string" their figures; then the children are ready to retell. (Adding a step of gluing the figures to cardstock rectangles or of laminating the figures will increase their life span.) Once the children have made books using your blackline master pages and are more skilled at filling a page with background, invite them to supply the coloring pages rather than using yours.

Where do backgrounds stop and characters begin? The younger the child, the fewer movable and losable figures there should be. Think of it in comparison to flannelgraph figures and backgrounds. Usually the flannel background is very simple, and there are many figures. In this case, consider merging minor figures with the background. For example, if the story is of David and Goliath, your first background page could include David's sheep with the landscape. David and his father are the loose figures. Simplify the retelling even further for very young children by making everyone in the story, except David, part of the background. Make all movable figures two-sided (an interesting task for children) so that the figures can enter and exit scenes.

Big books are another example of varying the presentation of a book. The Creation story lends itself to a group retelling in this format. The text may be extremely simple ("On the third day God made all the plants … On the fourth day God made the sun, moon, and stars") with the illustrations holding the attention. Show beautiful photographs of different types of sea creatures, plants, and land animals. The children can draw different ones, which they then cut out and glue to the page. Add your memory verse at the end if applicable. (I used Genesis 1:31 with my class.) Since the Creation story is often told at the beginning of the year, it's a simple introduction to retelling, it introduces ordinal numbers informally, and it bonds the class in a common project.

7

Depending on your input, the writing and illustrating of a big book, such as the Creation book, can be completed in one day or divided up and spread out over several days. The longest big book that our class made detailed daily the growth of brightly colored caterpillars from the day we discovered their eggs under a leaf until Christmas vacation—several weeks of gathering leaves and turning caterpillars loose on children's tables to observe them better and to measure them. Naturally the caterpillars had two aims—to get off those paper-covered open spaces and to get back to those delicious leaves—so measuring them was highly entertaining for everyone but the caterpillars. One finally stopped wiggling and went into a cocoon a few days before Christmas vacation. At that point we were all ready to write "The end" in our book.

For young children, the difficulty in making a book of any kind is often the time involved. Decrease the difficulty by using one or more of the following suggestions:

- Supply either the text or the illustrations.
- Offer smaller books with only three or four pages.
- Supply the background for the picture so that the child needs to draw only a few characters.
- Supply scenes to be cut and pasted in order.
- Use a rebus format with limited text and figures.
- Work in groups.
- Spread the project out over time.

Drama

7

We're all drawn to drama, both as input and as output. If your students are like mine, you've seen popular children's movies reenacted during every recess for weeks by students who were captivated by the story. In the beginning, children usually become the characters of the movie and follow the storyline closely (visual drama input to physical drama output). As time goes by, you may see them modify the replaying to add themselves as characters into the story and then to invent new episodes, moving out of story retelling into story creation.

Sometimes a dramatic retelling or replaying is a response to mental pictures created by words in a book or by a storyteller. Children aren't the only ones who are so inspired; think of the history buffs who reenact Civil War battles based on the historical accounts. If you are overseeing this type of retelling, your goal may be to have the retelling fairly exact but with a few advantageous, slight changes. For example, retelling Marcia Brown's *Stone Soup* (1947) story is much easier if at the right point in the story your "villagers" throw into the pot of cut-up vegetables a few bouillon cubes instead of raw chickens.

The first Bible curriculum we used had a unit on the boyhood of Jesus with the information presented as exposition rather than in story format. Instead of reading facts aloud as input, we acted out the situations—such as a family meal complete with stew and bread and a synagogue school for boys only, complete with scrolls, wax tablets, and skull caps, and with the girls having to stay in the house corner. The children did verbal retellings of the activity, and there was also creative dramatic output involved, since we modified the house corner for a day or two by taking out everything that wasn't part of that time and culture and adding clay jars, an oil lamp, mats, and other items. Notice the details that Bethany included in her story:

7

At Jesus' House
By Bethany

At one time they have a little house and they didn't have beds like ours. They had to roll the beds. And they had to put oil in the lights because they didn't have lights what we had. And they have to brought well water of the well. And then they had to wash their hands and they didn't have forks or spoons. And then when they was done they washed their hands again.

Drama and music go together easily. Music can supply structure, guiding the actions of the children as they listen carefully. Every time I've used music with children, there has been adult guidance. I used part of the *William Tell Overture* by Gioacchino Rossini to cue children as they acted out the story of William Tell, but I taught them the storyline and actions and made the final choice of actors for the different parts when we did it for their parents. The Scripture Press CD *Let's Sing Motions 'n Music*, which I used for several years, combines simple narration with musical interludes for the children to act out what was just narrated. The music directs the children's actions with its sounds of footsteps running, someone sitting down, someone swaying back and forth, and so on. (See the appendix for purchasing information for this CD.) I had to remind the children often that when the music stopped they needed to stop moving and giggling and to listen to the narrator again or they wouldn't know what to do next. If you're musically gifted, you could probably create your own musical stories. If you do this activity with the children often and the music and story are simple, children may be able to re-create the story through their motions without a great deal of guidance from you.

When the source of the words is children's previously recorded verbal retellings, adding drama (actors or puppets) calls attention to any gaps in the story and encourages children to retell the story more fully the next time or to add more to the story immediately. Making the story action and actors concrete enables children to catch on to the idea of narrative structure so that they can usually self-correct their stories. For variety, rather than reading a previously dictated script so that students respond to verbal cues, reverse the order; let a child describe what he sees the actors portraying. Another possibility is to record the story as the child retells it and as the actors follow his lead. Having actors in motion often prompts children to say more. (It's a good idea to record rather than type this because asking the child to repeat so that you can keep up kills the spontaneity.)

Another way to use drama to improve verbal retellings is to use a puppet that asks children to serve as actors in his story. The puppet "reads" his incomplete story aloud for the actors to perform. If you have a feisty puppet, he complains that the actors didn't act out the story correctly. If the children are taken aback, intervene on their behalf and tell the puppet he forgot to put those things in the story. Give the puppet a personality—whether blustering, shy, absentminded, or cheerfully unconcerned with details—and the children will be delighted to help him improve his story. It ends up being a group retelling as they discuss the puppet's story with him and help him improve it.

There is enough of a natural ham in most children that, given a few props, they can reenact or retell a story without a great deal of guidance. Expect the retelling to be less detailed if it is in response to a picture book or a storytelling session rather than a movie. Props don't need to be elaborate; there's usually something from your dress-up corner that will work. Create simple backgrounds of various colors using sheets or lengths of cloth (dark blue for night, light blue for daylight, brown for the inside of a simple house).

Finally, rather than using words, children can pantomime the story. One less-common use of pantomime for review is to let groups of students each pick a different story from among the ones they have

7

heard recently. Without telling anyone outside the group what the story is, they act it out for the class. Can their classmates guess which story they're acting out? Some groups need more guidance with this than others, especially the first time.

Retelling with Flannelgraph Figures

When you've told a story with flannelgraph figures, retelling with them follows naturally. The figures prompt recall and support organization, transforming review into playing school with the reteller in control. There are times when sharing the retelling role works better. As mentioned in the section about puppets, some young children falter when they need to coordinate telling with choosing and moving figures. Others, beguiled by the opportunity to move the figures, beg for the chance to stand up in front of the group, but once there they go blank with stage fright. Those for whom English is a foreign language may have a willing spirit, but they may find that expressing themselves is a challenge.

Sharing the retelling keeps children focused by allowing more children to participate. Whatever the reason, sometimes using the buddy system (pairing a speaker and a figure mover) or using successive retellers makes a retelling with flannelgraph figures flow more smoothly in a group setting. When teachers tell the story, they usually arrange the figures in a stack in order of their appearance in the story. For a child's retelling, I would usually spread out all the figures in order on a table in front of the board or on another flannelboard to one side so that all the choices were visible.

7

Placing figures in a center so that children can "play" with them afterward removes the pressure children may feel when they have to stand in front of the group to use them. There they can retell the story to dolls or to a classmate, or they can use a puppet as the audience or as the storyteller. It never ceases to fascinate me that children will speak directly to a puppet even when the teacher is obviously doing the talking for it. Even a very shy child may be persuaded to retell without self-consciousness or fear to a puppet—a mere piece of plastic whose head bobs occasionally and who offers a few encouraging words or pats.

If you are concerned that flannelgraph figures will be lost or torn if left in a center, make color copies of them, put a backing on the copies or laminate them, and build on the idea by Gibson, Gold, and Sgouros (2003) by making a small hole at the top of each one and attaching a long yarn tail. The tail can be draped over the top of the flannelboard, and the wool fibers in the yarn will help keep the figures in place. These tails also make lost figures easier to locate. The drawback to using copies, of course, is that the tactile pleasure of working with flannel figures is lost in the process.

Record the retelling occasionally for variety. An audiotape may be made during the group session or during center time and put in the listening center along with figures. Some background noise shouldn't be a problem if the goal is to encourage retelling rather than to produce a polished product. Videotaping the retelling is another possibility.

7

If you want more flexibility, create a narrated PowerPoint show. Take digital photos of the figures after a child places them on the board in scenes. Sometimes your picture may include the child, sometimes just the figures. Use the slide sorter view to put the pictures in order or to help the children put them in order. Show the pictures to the child narrator, and record her retelling the story as she views them. The third step is to combine the pictures and narration into one show (probably after the children are gone for the day). This PowerPoint show could also be done in two steps by inputting the narration directly into the show. Experiment to see which works best for you and your children.

Making Your Own Figures

Suppose you didn't use figures of the story characters during the input phase of telling the story, but you would like to use them during the retelling. Help children individually or as a class make their own flannelgraph figures, magnetic board figures, puppets, or action figures. Guide the children to think about what they know regarding each character in the story: Is he young or old? How can we show that? What type of clothes might she wear? There are two problems with making your own figures: first, drawing usable figures is often a problem for young children, and second, paper figures tend to curl or tear easily.

If your children tend to draw stick figures, try one of the following ideas:

- Thicken the stick figures by giving students thick markers, crayons, or a brush to draw the main outline. They can fill in the facial features and hair with a finer line afterward. (Model this process for them.) Help the children by drawing a cutting line—a rectangle or an outline that adds width.

- Another possibility is to show children how to construct figures from geometric shapes. Give each child a plain rectangle that is slightly larger than the size the figure will be. Provide a variety of precut shapes or give children cutting practice with your shape

7

drawings. Once they've created a recognizable figure with shapes, they can glue it to the background.

- Offer figures from a book of blackline masters, a coloring book, or clip art. Internet sites with coloring pages (see the resources in the appendix) usually allow you to make copies for your class. You could use the light setting on a photocopier to copy the flannelgraph figures from another story, since one bearded, middle-aged man in a robe looks very much like another. Again, draw the cutting line for children.

- Bring in a gingerbread man cookie cutter for them to trace or use as a stamp with a paint-covered sponge stamp pad. This will make an outline that they can fill in with clothing and features. Other possibilities are commercial paper cutouts of the same shape in different flesh tones, your own cutouts made with a hand-operated die-cut system, or stencils.

- Supply a drawing of clothing so that children need to add only arms, hands, legs, feet, and a circular head with facial features.

- Teach children to use a computer art program such as Kid Pix (see the appendix) to make figures, using the tool that makes the thickest line.

To deal with paper figures that are torn or curling (even laminated ones may curl), mount the figures on a stiff surface such as poster board, craft foam, or cardboard. Then, depending on how you plan to use the figures, to the back of them add magnets, flannel tape, the rough side of Velcro, clothespins, a fold-out stand, paper rings (for finger puppets), or whatever you need to finish them. Rather than using two-dimensional figures, consider using action figures, nativity figure sets, or tiny dolls and modify them as necessary (add yarn hair,

7

clothes made of cloth rectangles with a hole cut for the head, and thin elastic-type material for belts).

You can retell a story without a visual background, but do you want to pass up the opportunity to emphasize the setting? Discuss the background setting with the children. If your background will be made of paper, give children the thrill of tracing an outline projected onto a paper-covered wall. Or you could help them by either lightly sketching a general outline on the paper or simply guiding the artist's finger in a possible outline of a hill or a group of trees before the artist draws. If the background will be made of cloth such as flannel, the easiest solution is to buy commercial backgrounds and allow children to choose the appropriate one for the story. Another less-expensive option is to buy two pieces of flannel in solid colors (light blue for day, black for night) for the background, and rather than having children color on it, cut out shapes from flannel or felt that they can use to create a foreground. Use strong colors such as dark blue for water, yellow for sand, green for grassy areas, brown for barren ground. Check the resources in the appendix for websites that give directions for making felt figures and backgrounds if you would like to make your own.

Another reason for having children create backgrounds is to call attention to cultural differences and misunderstandings. You might think it would be obvious that a Bible story would not have cars or houses like ours in it; however, some families and churches have few resources and have not had the opportunity to show children storybooks or flannelgraph materials illustrating the stories. It is logical that the children would imagine the characters to be similar to themselves, and if the setting has unfamiliar elements, they unconcernedly add them to their mental representation of life. I recall a drawing by a boy who had just heard the story of Abraham moving from Ur. The child drew a tent. He told me it was Abraham's tent. It looked a great deal like a Bolivian house to me, complete with a Bolivian flag flying proudly in a stiff breeze out front. You couldn't fault his patriotism. Perhaps I should have spent more time talking about the setting of the story.

Rebus Stories

What child doesn't love chiming in during the reading of a rebus story? After reading a rebus story to the class to give them a model, suggest that the class create their own using a different story. As you plan for this activity, think through the following questions:

- Do you want the children to create the story individually, in small groups, or as a class?

- Do you want to begin with text or pictures, and where will you get them?

- Do you want to add a single sound effect (maybe sheep bleating), replace a single word (such as *sling* or the character name *David*), or replace several different words in the same story (*sling*, *David*, *Saul*, and *Jonathan*)?[1]

- Do you want to use each child's drawing of the same figure (15 versions of David), or do you want to give everyone the same figure to color?

- Do you want the final story to be displayed as a paper book, a wall display, or a form of technology?

7

---

[1] The Jewish celebration of Purim includes an audience participation activity that reminds me of rebus stories. When the book of Esther is read aloud (with no pictures, so it isn't a rebus story, but you can imagine the possibilities), the people in the audience cheer whenever the names of Mordecai and Esther are read, and they boo, hiss, or use noisemakers whenever Haman's name is read.

A factor to consider with rebus stories is how many times a particular word will be repeated in the story. If you want every child to contribute a picture, think of how many substitutions you can make in one story. You may solve this by using the extra pictures elsewhere (in a decorative border or on a title page), by having the children take turns supplying pictures (if you repeat the activity often), or by splitting into groups.

Do you want to instruct children to draw the pictures first and then create the story? In the following example, the teacher asked the children to make drawings of sheep, and then she used them to help the children create a retelling of a story:

Teacher I like the pictures of sheep that you made. Why did I ask you to make a sheep and not a giraffe or a rhinoceros?

Child Because David had sheep.

Teacher Yes, he did. Can you help me tell the story? I'm going to write, "David took care of his father's." (The teacher writes the words while saying them aloud, and then turns back to the children.)

Child Teacher, you forgot to say *sheep*.

Teacher I did, didn't I? Instead of writing the word, can two people let me put their sheep there?

Everyone You can use mine!

Teacher	(Teacher continues once two sheep are in place.) What did David do for his sheep in our story?
Child	He took them to eat grass.
Teacher	Yes, he did. Now, I can write it just like that, "He took them to eat grass" or, so that I can use some more sheep pictures, I could write …
Child	I know, I know! "He took his *sheep* to eat grass." Can I put my sheep up?

Once they catch on, it goes fairly easily. If you run out of sheep or have some left over, ask the children how they think you can solve this problem.

If you begin with the text—in either a class retelling or an individual retelling—and you didn't tell the children that it would be used as a rebus story, they may want to change some pronouns to nouns when you replace words with pictures. In the story by Michelle in chapter 1, she uses *David* or *David's* twelve times, *Saul* or *King Saul* three times, and *Jonathan* four times. If you wanted a few more pictures of Saul and Jonathan, some pronouns could be changed, but you may not want to tamper with her storytelling style.

What will be the source of your pictures and text? Do you want to use individual stories or group stories, or do you want to supply at least part of the story as an example in the beginning? Do you want children to draw the pictures themselves, or do you want to give them the figures to color? Suppose that you are replacing only the word *David*. Everyone knows that no matter how much the children's

7

117

drawings differ, they are all of David. Forestall problems by explaining that we don't have any photographs or paintings made of David when he was alive, so no one knows exactly what he looked like. The Bible does tell us in 1 Samuel 16:12 that he was "ruddy," meaning that his skin and hair were more reddish than brown or black and that he had "beautiful eyes and a handsome appearance." Assure the children that it is okay if their pictures are a little different from each other's because, remember, we don't have any real pictures of him. But everyone should try to make his hair reddish (discuss what marker or crayon to use to get a color that everyone agrees on), his eyes beautiful (which probably means they'll be big and wide open with eyelashes), and his general appearance handsome (ask, "How could we draw him to try to make him look handsome, children?"). It's up to you whether or not you want them to copy another person's drawing to make their pictures more similar.

If you are replacing the bears and Goldilocks in the story *The Three Bears* (1965), the bears have to differ from each other fairly consistently and your students may insist that the figures look the same each time. You could use commercially drawn pictures, but if you are utterly opposed to using commercial coloring book figures, ask for volunteers to draw the figures from the story. Maybe Pammi will draw an outline picture of Goldilocks, Matthew of Papa Bear, Ingrid of Mother Bear, and Carlos of Baby Bear. Cut a sheet of paper into quarters, and give one to each of the four children to draw on. When the children finish their blackline drawings, photocopy as many copies as you need and distribute them to the class for coloring. If the story text is already done, you know how many copies of each figure are needed. To make sure that Goldilocks' dress is the same color throughout the adventure or that Baby Bear remains black or brown throughout the story, discuss this detail with the class members and encourage them to decide on the basic colors and perhaps sit together while coloring, to help them remember.

If you're looking for a reinforcement activity that children can do at home with their parents, make copies of the group story and leave space for children to add the pictures. Using the idea in the previous paragraph, shrink the pictures small enough to fit on small, square-shaped labels available in office supply stores and print them, either as a grouping (maybe five pictures of Goldilocks, three of Papa Bear and Mama Bear, and four of Baby Bear) or as separate sheets (one sheet of Goldilocks labels and another of each of the bears) that you cut apart. However you decide to organize your labels, cut the sheets so that each child has a set of child-created stickers with which to finish the story at home. In your take-home instructions, ask parents to first read the story aloud to their child, have their child insert the stickers in the proper places, and then reread it together so that their child can participate in the story. Perhaps after a time or two the parent and child can switch roles. Even if the child doesn't retell the story exactly the way it is written, the parent can still manage to chime in at the proper place. Also in your instructions, mention how the pictures and story were created so that no parent feels slighted or feels inclined to criticize the artwork because their child wasn't the illustrator this time.

What will the finished rebus story look like? You might choose chart paper with the text on it and cover the words with the pictures. Or the chart paper could have sentence strips that enable you to cut out the words and insert the pictures. You may want to set the cutout words aside so that later you can ask the children to match the words to the pictures. If you create a book version of this, you might adapt

7

the interactive book idea and put the words on the end of ribbons to match to the pictures.

Small-Group or Paired Retellings

Small-group or paired retellings hover between group and individual retellings. Again, having an adult nearby provides structure that your students may need. Using flannelgraph figures or a picture book, so that the retelling is part of playing teacher, provides similar structure. A signal, such as a bell or timer, to change speakers reminds students to give another person a turn. In the following example, the children chose their groups and their speaking order, and I typed their retelling. Because it was this group's first experience with a group retelling, I suggested when to change speakers. See if you can pinpoint where the speakers changed:

David Cares for His Sheep
By Hugo, Stevie, and Marcos

David was the youngest boy in his family. One day a lion came up and David got up and took his stick. He kill the lion and he drop the lion on the dirt. Then a bear came den he took a sheep. Den David took a stick then he hit him two times. Then he killed him, then he died. The sheep was so happy because the bear and the lion were dead. Den he care the sheeps den was a happy day thank for God keeping the sheeps so nobody can take one the sheeps and eat 'em.

CHAPTER 8

Additional Uses for Retellings

Is retelling finished when a child finishes his last sentence or last paint stroke? Technically, yes, but teachers are famous for scrutinizing every activity for multiple uses and squeezing the last bit of value out of everything. Retelling is no exception. We're all expected to provide work samples to support assessment, and we're all expected to share with other classes and parents what our class has learned. In this chapter we'll look at the use of retellings to document progress in informal and formal collections of work, to measure improvement in story structure and language, and to share the class' learning through displays that showcase the charm of preschool expression.

Collections of Work and Portfolios

Retellings fit well in both informal collections of student work and in more structured portfolios. Whichever you decide to use, take care to date all retellings. Students love to do this. Set the date correctly on a date stamp or provide a model of the day's date and the correct number stamps for each of the numerals represented in the date. Teach the students to draw a box in the upper right-hand corner of the page before they begin their picture and to stamp the date in that box. (I felt that stamping the date three or four times dead center

8

detracted from the finished product, but not all kindergartners agreed with me.) If you want to compare stories for progress, make sure that the stories you compare are similar in structure and difficulty. Knowing whether a particular story was supported with visuals during the input phase and how much help was given during output also helps make comparisons more reliable.

Typing a retelling exactly as it is said—with all the "dats" and "deys"—allows the teacher to note improvement in pronunciation over a period of time. Often, differences from standard speech, such as "dat" for "that," are minor and correct themselves. There are times, however, when a child's speech is difficult to understand and you ask yourself why that is. Having the retelling written down in black and white sometimes clarifies problems. Does a child need her attention drawn to the endings of words or to particular sounds? Do you need to speak more clearly? Is the speech problem resulting from a muddling of languages? One of my students, Reina, spoke Japanese with her parents, was learning Spanish to speak with her Bolivian relatives, and was now struggling to learn English in school. Her speech was difficult to understand at times, and she had trouble identifying common sounds in the environment as well. Was this an indication that intervention of some kind was necessary, or was this something she would self-correct as she became more fluent in English? I didn't know, but I gave the principal a copy of the following story so that it could be sent to the school she would be attending in Japan the next year:

Noah and the Ark
By Reina

God said boos he comin stwaa woo. Woos is gooman an he listeGod said. God said it conna stwaa woo. Woos make a big boat. He pick a aimals a mommy an' a daddy. Woos take lion aehan bears. Efans, horsies, bunnies, birds.

Translation: God said soon he coming start flood [or is it *water* or *wood*—it sounded like *wood* without the *d*]. Woos [Ruth?—an earlier story] is good man and he listen God said. God said it gonna start flood/water/wood. Woos make a big boat. He pick the animals—a mommy and a daddy. Woos take lion and a bears. Elephants, horsies, bunnies, birds.

Most teachers collect work samples to review with parents at parent-teacher conferences, to display, or to trigger their memory of student progress when writing reports. When I visited Romanian kindergartens, teachers would pull out individual student folders with every paper (mostly art) done during the year kept neatly in order—obviously they didn't do busywork sheets. If you keep a folder of papers for each child, at some point you may decide to make each child a portfolio—a smaller, more permanent selection that is representative of that child's progress.

Portfolios designed to showcase student achievement are usually more organized and exclusive than folders of papers. They often contain a table of contents and are organized according to time or learning goals. They may be focused on one area of development such as the development of literacy, or they may be more general in scope. The downside is that this type of organization requires more planning than merely slipping sample papers into folders when the urge hits you. If the thought of bulky folders discourages you, consider scanning student work or photographing it and saving it on computer disks if you have the technology available. Adult volunteers or student aides can help. Older students are often involved in evaluating their own

8

work, using rubrics and choosing the work that is kept. They also can maintain their portfolios independently. Some writers of education materials believe that even young students can learn to evaluate their work if given sufficient guidance; therefore, these writers believe that children should have a part in what is included in their portfolios.

Whether or not you involve young children in maintaining their portfolios, the aim is to keep an organized record of student progress. Retellings can be included to show attention to detail, expressiveness, understanding and mastery of material, grasp of story or expository structure, improvement in language acquisition, and progress in literacy foundations. Making a note, even if only a brief one, as to why a paper is included in a collection or portfolio saves you time later when you open the work folder and wonder why you kept particular pieces.

Measuring Improvement

Informal Evaluations

If you choose to score the stories to note improvement or areas of need, there are a number of different ways to do this, depending on your aims. These range from informal notes to more precise scoring measures.

Brown and Cambourne (1987) suggest using informal evaluation of the retelling process, and of the finished product, to note how much understanding upper-elementary school students have of what they read, how much structure there is in their written retelling, and how well they use the conventions of spelling, punctuation, and grammar.

8

In early education, our concern revolves around how well our children understand what they hear, how well they recall it, and how they use language and structure to communicate these achievements through their retelling. Affective factors matter to us as well. We want this introduction to the written word and the power and enjoyment it offers children to be positive.

Informal records of content may be as simple as a note attached to a retelling, for example, "Jason included all of the characters and most of the details of the story." We might use an arrow or a colored dot to call attention to a particular part of the retelling that stands out. One of my favorites was one child's version of Saul's words when David appeared at the battle lines: "Hey, I know you! You're the guy that plays the harp!" Indicators of emotional reaction, such as "Carl spoke more loudly and confidently," help you gauge affect. As children retell, keep alert for anxiety and look for ways to relieve it. Give the needed support because in the long run a child's attitude toward school, literacy, subject matter, and the people involved matters far more than the child's short-term recall of the content of a few stories.

Story Structure and Completeness

Rubrics are another way to focus attention on the elements of a retelling. Some rubrics list the desired behaviors and ask raters to indicate with a check mark how the criteria are met. The following chart shows the easiest type of rubric to create:

8

Chart 2

Parts of retelling	Without prompting	With prompting	Not included
Names of main characters			
Names of supporting characters			
Description of setting			
Main episodes			
Problem and solution			
Application			

If you use this type of rubric, scoring will be much easier if you make a written note of the information you want to see included, such as the names of each of the characters. When you are preparing to tell the story, make a habit of including on your scoring sheet master the names of all characters, the setting description, and other elements that you will include in your telling and that you expect to hear during the retelling.

Some rubrics will list descriptive behaviors for each category, and they often include a numerical point system, such as that found in the following chart:

8

Chart 3	Criteria			
	3	**2**	**1**	**Points**
Main characters (or characters)	Uses correct names and correct descriptions	Uses incorrect names, correct descriptions	Uses incorrect names and descriptions, or does not mention	
Supporting characters	Mentions all or most by appropriate names	Mentions at least half	Mentions fewer than half	
Problem or Goal	Correctly states	Does not mention	Incorrectly states	

This second type of rubric is more time-consuming and difficult to create. For example, it may be easy to divide the category of main character into three descriptors, but a statement of the problem may not lend itself to this as readily and you may want to modify the categories after you use the chart a few times. Some educators propose that the teacher use the rubric to discuss a student's work with the student. Whether or not you feel this is appropriate depends on the age of your students and your purpose in having students retell.

Another way to keep track of story completeness, comprehension, or story structure is to create a check sheet of the structural elements of the story—such as the number of characters, the setting, the main events, and the closing—so that you know what you're looking for. Naturally you will make sure that you include all these parts when you tell the story if you are expecting to hear them in retellings of the story. After the retelling, compare the child's retelling to this checklist and staple the two together. Note how the following checklist tracks Tommy's story:

8

Chart 4

Story Structure and Elements for <u>Jeremiah Speaks for God</u>

Date: *August* 28

Name: *Tommy*

Characters:

✓ Jeremiah (main character)

✓ God

✓ people (Israelites)

✓ kind man (Ebed-melech)

__ king (Zedekiah)

Setting: not given by teacher

Problem or Goal:

✓ tell people about God

Plot Episodes:

✓ God says to tell

✓ people angry and throw in well

✓ Jeremiah sinks into the mud

__ kind man asks king to let him rescue

✓ rescues Jeremiah, takes home

Resolution:

✓ Jeremiah continues to preach

8

Jeremiah Speaks for God

By Tommy

One day God told Jeremiah to go to tell the people about Him but the people did not like it so they threw him in a deep hole with mud in the bottom of it and he got stuck way deep in the mud. But then a nice man came and tied cloths together and told him to put them under his arms. Then the nice man took him to his house and took care of him. But Jeremiah did not quit telling them that they should obey God and quit doing bad things. But most of the times they did not like it.

The easiest way to score a story similar to the previous example is to check the elements that are present. If you want to give each of them a numerical value so that you can compare story structure with other retellings, award one point for each main element mentioned. In the case of supporting characters and plot episodes, divide those named by the total possible to get a percentage.

You can also compare individual progress over time in these areas.

Chart 5

Kate								
Retelling date, story	T-units	Intro	Main characters	Supporting characters	Setting	Problem or Goal	Plot episodes	Resolution
8/28, Jeremiah	9.2	0	1	1	0	1	1	1
9/19, Daniel	8.5	0	1	1	0	1	1	1
10/2, Lot	13.5	0	1	.2	0	0	.3	0

You may be interested in the progress of the class as a whole.

8

Chart 6

Story: Jeremiah Speaks for God						Date: 8/28		
	T-units	Intro	Main characters	Supporting characters	Setting	Problem or Goal	Plot episodes	Resolution
Maria	2.8	0	1	.25	0	1	.8	1
Carter	8	1	1	1	0	1	1	1
Tommy	13	1	1	.75	0	1	.8	1
Marcos	3.6	0	1	.25	0	1	.2	0
Christy	8.1	0	1	1	0	.5	1	1

Scoring retellings in early education often highlights areas of need or achievement for teachers as well as students. After evaluating the preceding partial listing of class scores, I had to ask myself, "Do I need to make a clear verbal statement of setting rather than assuming that children will get this from the visuals?" I saw that most of these students recalled the goal and the resolution, and they correctly recounted the basic facts of the story.

When children are retelling Bible stories, correct factual recall is only part of the goal. Head knowledge without heart knowledge and life application is incomplete. Some scoring methods that measure "richness of retelling" (Moss 2004) ask whether the student has made a statement of application in the retelling. Young children are more likely than older children to omit this in their retellings because it is not essential to the drama of the story. Those who are familiar with the story are more likely to latch onto your application as something new and interesting and add it to their retellings, particularly if you weave it into the story. In the following story, note how Chris included the detail that "Jesus is never late":

8

Jesus and Jairus' Daughter
By Chris

There was lot of people around Jesus. And someone ran and his name was Jairus. And he needed to push all the crowd around to get to Jesus 'cause he went to the daughter and the daughter was really sick. And Jesus said, "I will come." So he went and people—he was close to his house—and people was coming out of his house sad and they were crying because one man came up to Jairus and said, "Your daughter is dead so you don't bother Jesus anymore." But they thought Jesus was late, but Jesus is never late. So he went to the house and only her mother and father and two disciples and Jesus in the room and Jesus took her hand and said, "Get up, little girl!" And so she got up and ran around the room and not too long she could run and play and skip and play with her friends.

If asked about the main point or the application, many will answer correctly, even if you did not specifically mention it in the story. I recall overhearing a conversation between a visitor and Bonnie, a child from a non-Christian family. Bonnie had been in school for only three months. The visitor asked our young artist about her picture of the lost sheep and then asked how people are like the lost sheep in the story. To my surprise, Bonnie answered correctly. Clearly, she had been listening during the previous story when David likened himself to a sheep and God to his Shepherd; however, as you can see from her retelling, that application is missing:

8

The Lost Sheep
By Bonnie

Once there was a shepherd who had a hundred sheep. There was a mommy one, a daddy one, and a baby one. And he loved the sheep. An' then there was a little lamb called Snowflake and he didn't want to listen to the shepherd. An' den Snowflakes saw a nice green, grassy place and he went there and the shepherd said, "Snowflakes, come here with the rest of us." An' so little Snowflakes said to him, "Oh well, I'll go," but inside himself he said that next time I'm going to go somewhere where you can't see me. And den he went in the grassy place and started eating and eating until he got farther and farther away from the shepherd and his flock. An' then when he got there he started eating and eating and it got a little bit dark. And then little Snowflake, "Ah! I have to go home with the other flock!" And den he was looking through one way and the other and it was not right. And den little Snowflake fell down in a hole with lots of thorns. And then he started, "Baaaaa," and the shepherd couldn't hear him. An' then the shepherd came by and was calling, "Snowflakes, where are you?" An' den da shepherd went by and found him and den da shepherd moved the thorns and tried to get deep inside the hole. And then the shepherd took him out of the hole and carried him home.

Combining retelling with questioning and discussion brings out important information. Scoring a retelling has its uses. Keep your ultimate goals in mind, however, so that your understanding of a young child's learning and growth isn't reduced to a set of numbers that may or may not accurately represent reality.

8

Language

If you are interested in language complexity you can score a retelling for "T-units," or "minimal terminable units" (Hunt 1965). This is probably not something you want to do every week or even every month, but doing it two to four times a year will give you an idea of children's growth. Researchers consider these reliable measures of the complexity of a child's language, although in some cases children become verbose without becoming complex. One T-unit equals a main clause and any subordinate clauses. "He went to sleep because he was tired" is one T-unit. A compound sentence such as "He went to sleep, and he had a dream" is two T-units. To score a retelling, divide it into T-units, count the total number of words, and then divide that number by the number of T-units to get an average. Researcher Walter Loban (1966) said that the average for kindergarten children who discussed what they saw in a series of pictures ranged between 4 and 6 words per T-unit. Most of my students scored higher than this, probably because they had a model; instead of generating a new story, they were recalling a story and language that they had heard recently.

You will notice that with the story by Kaito, dividing the story into units involves some guessing since he leaves out words. In his study on the writing of older students, researcher Kellogg W. Hunt (1965) uses the term *garbles* for groups of words that aren't understandable to the scorer of that piece of writing, and he eliminates them before scoring. I left them in and made the best guess I could as to meaning. The following is a story divided into T-units:

8

February 21
Jesus Heals a Leper
By Kaito

Man is sick. / Man … hand / man is walk / and everybody don't touch man. / Everybody say, "Don't touch me." / And everybody say, "I don't gave you presents." / And Jesus touch yucky man / and Jesus say, "I will like you." / And yucky man say, "Look at my hand and feet well. / My feet clean up." / And Jesus like fast man and skinny man / and yucky man, pretty man, and good man Jesus like. / And with good man is back 'is house.

[79 words divided by 13 T-units equals 6 words per T-unit.]

In comparing this story to Kaito's first story of the year about Saul's conversion, his story that consisted of "Saul … God … Bible … God … praying to God … Saul died," the improvement in language and content is clear. Kaito's T-unit score in this case was 1.5.

You might want to compare the total number of words per story over time and the percentage of different words, as shown in the following chart. In the case of Kaito, as his knowledge of English grew over the year, his confidence and ability to retell a story increased. Some cases provide more obvious results than do others.

Chart 7

Date	Total number of words	Number of different words	Percentage of different to total	T-units
Sep 10	9	6	66	1.5
Oct 25	70	31	44	4.1
Feb 21	79	34	43	6.0
Apr 8	148	61	41	5.3

8

Looking more closely at a child's use and misuse of the various parts of speech helps the teacher pinpoint areas of need for that child. The following chart, based on a modified version of Loban's list of errors (1966) and Kaito's story, clarifies some of these areas of need:

Chart 8

Text [partial story]	Subject-verb agreement	Verb tense, form	Omissions	Pronouns	Nouns, possessives	Prepositions, conjunctions	Adjectives, adverbs	Word order
Man is sick.		was	the					
Man … hand. [The man hurt his hand?]*			the, hurt, his					
man is walk.		was walking	the					
and everybody don't touch man.		touched	the	no-body				
Everybody say, "Don't touch me."		said						
And everybody say, "I don't gave you presents." [I won't help you?]*		said, won't help	any		presents doesn't fit			
And with good man is back 'is house.		went	the	his		with (not necessary), to		

* Unclear

What is he doing well? He's expanding his vocabulary. He's using more complex speech than earlier in the year. He's communicating the story well. Focusing on adding the article *the* to nouns and introducing the word *nobody* and using the past tense "was" could be targeted with him, or even the class as a whole if a number of children have similar problems in English. After you provide instruction and practice in a particular area, reevaluate to gauge whether you were successful.

Before moving on, let me reiterate that the decision about whether to score retellings is a matter of personal choice. Before portfolios were popular, I collected retellings in individual student folders for years without ever scoring them. I then started scoring them, but after several years, I went back to not scoring them. At that point I collected them in individual student folders and used them in assorted ways. It's helpful to have options from which you can choose.

Sharing Retellings

Much of the charm of retelling is in sharing it with others so that they can appreciate the unique perspective of a preschooler. Unfortunately, not everyone is as understanding of this technique and as enraptured by it as you are. If you are typing the stories exactly as they are dictated, there will be times when the grammar and spelling will not match Standard English. Make the reasoning behind doing this clear to parents so that they don't lose confidence in your spelling and grammar skills. There were occasions when the children themselves realized that what I was reading back didn't sound the way they expected it to sound. If a child can read and is reading along as you type, he may notice that the typing doesn't match what he knows to be correct. I had one young reader point out that I'd typed "dat" instead of "that." I told him that he had said it that way, but then I asked whether he would like to say it differently. He frowned in concentration and then carefully pronounced it correctly thereafter. In his case he had developed speech habits that he was ready and able to overcome. If you feel it is demeaning not to "clean up" retellings, there is nothing to stop you from typing the correct spellings.

Several other uses of retellings have been mentioned already. Obviously they are wonderful raw material for displays both inside and outside the classroom. Offer students from other classes the challenge of putting unlabeled, out-of-order scenes from a familiar story back in order on a bulletin board or similar display outside your room. (How much of a challenge it is may have more to do with the quality of the drawings than with knowledge of the story's sequence.) How well do parents recognize their child's speech patterns? At Back-to-School Night, can they find their child's retelling from a stack of unnamed retellings and match it to their child's self-portrait?

When I taught second grade, my class was put in charge of one chapel service each semester. Because this was before the days of video recorders, we retold the story of Noah using a cassette tape player and a slide show with the class members as Noah and the other characters in the story. Today it could be done much more easily with a video recorder or with PowerPoint and either photos or scanned pictures of the story. Times have changed.

School newspapers, parent newsletters, class Web pages, class books … the possible uses of student retellings go on and on. Get all the mileage that you can out of your students' retellings.

8

CHAPTER 9

Benefits of Using Retelling

You already have methods and curriculum in place that work well for you. Is it worth the effort to add retelling to your repertoire of methods? Most of us are continually on the lookout for new ideas that will work well with our students and our resources and that will result in learning rather than just filling time. I hope that by this point in the book you've found at least one or two ideas you can use or adapt. In order to further encourage you, in this chapter we will be considering how retelling promotes student learning and supports your professional growth.

Benefits for Students

The following are several areas in which retelling provides support for children's development:

- **Letters, sounds, words, and concepts of print.** One of the main benefits of using retelling in early education is the informal exposure it provides to children of the connection between speaking, reading, and writing through concrete experiences, interaction with adults, and adult modeling. This exposure includes practice with the letters, sounds, and words that the children are learning, as well as with the concepts they are forming about print and its use.

• **Story structure.** Whether story structure is taught directly or indirectly, gaining an understanding of text or story structure through retelling is another part of learning to read, because this knowledge helps children approach reading material with expectations that aid their understanding and recall.

• **Vocabulary and language complexity.** A third part of moving children along the path of literacy involves helping them develop vocabulary and language complexity through retelling.

• **Recall and comprehension.** Retelling also aids in recall and comprehension of the information that is stored in a child's bank of knowledge and experience.

• **Personal responsibility and focused attention.** Another benefit of retelling, less directly connected with the development of literacy but still important, is the responsibility that children take for their learning.

• **A sense of accomplishment.** Another important benefit is the pride and sense of accomplishment that children experience in their achievement.

Letters, Sounds, Words, and Concepts of Print

During individual retellings I typed each story in a large easy-to-read font so that the children could see their words appearing on the screen as they stood beside me and dictated their story. Often they would stop their story to comment on a particular letter or on words such as *God* (which they recognized from seeing it appear fairly often in their weekly memory verse[1]) or *Daniel* (if there happened to be someone named Daniel in the class that year).

Zaccheus
By Lucas

One day there was one man that he call Zaccheus an' he have a *Z*. And he have a lot, a lot, a lot of money. Den he was so happy to see Jesus. He was short and the other tall people don't let him see. An' den der was one tree an' Zaccheus climbed to the tree. An' Jesus walk and say to Zaccheus, "Zaccheus, come down. I going to go to your house to eat." Den Zaccheus was too excited. Den when too many he give one to the poor and he stayed with one. "Den I have two shirt, I give one to the poor and one stay with me. I have two dogs, one to the poor and one to me." That's all.

Some children found it intensely interesting to see their words appear in print. Others either hadn't reached that level of involvement with print yet or were concentrating so hard on their story recall or oral language that stopping to notice written language was out of the question.

During group retellings, individual responsibility is lessened, but children are still exposed to literacy components as they watch you print contributions on chart paper or on the chalkboard. Some students (or the teacher) may comment on the written language, calling everyone's attention to different elements such as left-to-right

---

[1] I printed their memory verse in three-inch letters on poster board and used it for various language-related activities in addition to its primary use in learning the verse and reviewing it.

9

progression (note that this can be present in a nonverbal retelling as well), letter formation, spacing, and punctuation.

Seeing their words written and later hearing them read aloud helps children appreciate the function and value of written language. Our school was blessed to have a principal who had taught in both preschool and the primary grades. She occasionally dropped in and obligingly made a point of reading aloud some of the displayed work of the children (they watched with bated breath to see if she got it right) and praising them while they grinned and giggled with pleasure. When they took their stories home, many parents would read the stories aloud, further demonstrating written language's function in preserving thoughts and words.

Story Structure

Much of the research on retelling has focused on its effect on memory and on the understanding of material. Early research centered on how the verbal rehearsal of material affected the remembrance of it. As you can imagine from having done verbal rehearsal yourself to remember phone numbers and short grocery lists, the research showed that saying something aloud helps people remember it later. Some researchers, though, were interested in more than just the recall of lists. Jean M. Mandler and Nancy S. Johnson (1977), from the University of California, began examining the effect of story structure on children's recall of a story. Their classic article, "Remembrance of Things Parsed: Story Structure and Recall," drew attention to the importance of structure in the successful recall (measured by retelling) of a story. Continuing the cycle, the active involvement of children, through their verbal rehearsal of that recall (retelling), promotes an increased sense of story structure for them (Morrow 1990).

Do you want to directly teach children to recognize and use story structure, or are you more comfortable teaching this indirectly? Sometimes we get the impression that any direct teaching is bad because it interferes with natural development. Our language curriculum included a thinking skills component. In one activity, the teacher drew a picture of a man beforehand and kept it hidden from the children. The teacher instructed them to ask questions about the man in the picture—such as "Does he have hair?" and "Is it curly?"—in order to discover what the hidden figure looked like. They drew their version of the teacher's picture, detail-by-detail, on the basis of the information they discovered. When they felt that they had asked enough questions and had drawn the figure correctly, the teacher unveiled hers and everyone compared theirs with hers. Round head, square head, curly hair, straight hair, ears, no ears, round eyes, oval eyes, two eyes, three eyes, round body, stick body—there were unlimited options. I used this activity for several years, following the directions given in the teacher manual. My students knew what a human body looked like, and they used that knowledge, gradually becoming more skilled in asking questions. Then one year I had an aide who was an artist. After her first opportunity to observe the children as they asked their random questions during this activity, she huddled with them and suggested that they start with questions about the top of the body and work their way down rather than asking questions about whatever came to their minds. This strategy had the effect of "sharpening the edge of the ax" (as in Ecclesiastes 10:10). Their questions became more focused, and the game went faster and was more fun for all of us. Some of the children already had been unconsciously using that strategy, but when she made it explicit, everyone benefited.

I never taught story structure directly; it never occurred to me to do so. As we did retellings over the year, the different activities gave children

9

practice in using story structure, and those who didn't already use it began doing so. Perhaps because I didn't emphasize that they needed to use story structure, the children didn't use it all the time, even after they had demonstrated that they knew how to retell a well-structured story. Cathy was a sociable and strong-willed child. The stories I have from her follow an interesting pattern. One story from October shows an excellent use of story structure. Then in November she apparently became more fascinated with the social relationships in stories rather than with the story line. She managed to include the mention of the lions in the story of Daniel, but just barely:

Daniel in the Lions' Den
By Cathy

Der was a when they frew Daniel in the lions 'cause he didn't obey the law. And he didn't. He prayed each morning and each night to God. But he never obeyed the mean servants. He never did 'cause he wanted to obey God. But why didn't he obey the king? 'Cause he didn't want to obey the king. He didn't like obeying kings. The king was his friend but almost always the servants of the king are trying to trick him. Why did they want to trick him? He hadn't done anything to them. That's all.

A month later, in her story of the wise men's visit to baby Jesus, she got a little more of the story in, but Jesus never made an appearance. She was still getting sidetracked, this time by the familiar social situation of visiting a home to admire a new baby and give a carefully chosen gift:

The Wise Men
By Cathy

There was some men that knew all the star's names. One night while they were doing something an' they saw one beautiful star that they had never seen before and so they thought and thought and thought an' one had a good idea that a baby was born and then one of them said, "What should we give him?" One of them found out a good idea—jewelry! The other was thinking and said, "I know! Nice perfume!" And the different one said, "I know where baby kings are born. They're born in palaces." And then they went ta a palace an' they locked up the door an' said, "A new king is born. Can we please come in and see the new king?" And then the maid went to tell her boss, and then the boss came out and said, "Come in," and so they did and that's all.

Two and a half months later, she showed the same tendency to dive into the social morass, but this time she seemed to catch herself in the midst of her musings and finish the story:

Jesus Heals a Leper
By Cathy

There was a man that had leprosy and everyone said, "Shoo, go away!" But Jesus didn't say shoo, go away. But the others did say shoo, go away. But Jesus didn't even bother to say shoo, go away. So Jesus was talking with some people an' the man that had leprosy came along and the other people said, "Shoo, go away." But Jesus didn't say shoo, go away. Jesus said dat he would make da man well. "Surely, surely," Jesus said, "that I will heal you." An' because Jesus healed him 'cause Jesus loved him.

9

After this she went back to using story structure to guide her retellings. Even in the story of the prodigal son, in places where she could have either digressed into her waffling or gotten embroiled in the son's social calendar, she stayed on track and retold the story well. Knowing how to use story structure doesn't ensure that a child will consistently use it, but by the end of the year all my students were using story structure consistently.

Vocabulary and Language Complexity

Children come to preschool or kindergarten with a wide range of language skills. Some children are simply more linguistically gifted than others. At the other end of the continuum are those whose gifts and experience make functioning in "school language" a challenge for them, even when the school language is their native tongue. Some children in our programs know their mother tongue well, but we teach in what is for them a second or third foreign language. One of our major goals should be to build on the language development that has already taken place at home or to support their learning of a new language.

I don't think any of us doubt the importance of the home in language development. At one point I correlated children's retellings with results from a questionnaire that asked the parents when they began reading to their child and how often they did so. I found, as you would expect, that the children with more exposure to reading—whose parents had begun reading to them early (before their second birthday) and did so often—demonstrated more use of story structure, more richness of detail, and more language complexity in their retellings than the children whose parents did not read to them as often. We're glad for children who come from language-rich homes, but what about the others? We have no control over what has happened in the past.

We're more interested in what practices we can use in the classroom to help them now. I don't think there are any quick fixes and easy answers. Will using retelling by itself magically increase the language complexity and richness of expression for all your students? No, of course it won't; but then, it is never "by itself," is it?

Educator and author Lesley Mandel Morrow (1985) suggests that practice in retelling improves children's language complexity in retellings. That is what we would expect to happen. Practice, which increases familiarity with a task, usually results in improvement. This is particularly true when children begin kindergarten at a low level in their language development. Those who begin at a high level, such as Abby, are less likely to show marked improvement over the year:

September 3
Jeremiah Preaches
By Abby

Once upon a time a long time ago there lived a man named Jeremiah. Jeremiah spoke to God with his mouth. One time God spoke to Jeremiah, "Jeremiah, I want you to go tell the people this." Jeremiah was afraid to do it. So then he went and told the people. The people didn't like what Jeremiah said. One morning they were so angry with Jeremiah that they threw him down into a deep, dark hole. Down, down, down he went. It was all muddy at the bottom. One morning a servant came and wrapped some rags around Jeremiah and pulled him out of the well. The servant took Jeremiah home and kept him in his own house. The next time when God spoke to Jeremiah, Jeremiah went. I don't know any more.

9

Another child, Sharon, showed progress that is more typical of native English speakers. Her progress over the year is documented by the following stories:

September
Jeremiah Preaches
By Sharon

Jeremiah went over to preach and he went over to and then they throw him in a big well and then someone helped him out.

November
Daniel in the Lions' Den
By Sharon

One day there was a king and there was some jealous men that tricked the king and the bad men said, "I love you, King," and Daniel sat down in his window to pray and the jealous men saw him and threw him into the lions' den.

March
The Mount of Transfiguration
By Sharon

Once upon a time, long, long ago there was Jesus and three of his disciples. And then they were going, they were climbing up a mountain and then finally they got up to the top of the mountain and His disciples just went to sleep. And then He, and then after they woke up they saw Jesus and Moses and Elijah. And then ... [Sharon lost concentration at this point for some reason and kept repeating "and then, and then, and then," which the transcriber started to record. This caught Sharon's attention, and she questioned it. When the transcriber explained, she protested, "Don't put that in there!"] And then they saw, they saw Jesus and Moses and Elijah. And they were bright, bright, bright and they couldn't look at. And the three disciples couldn't look at them. And then a cloud came over 'um, and then the cloud passed away and Jesus was only left. A voice came out of the cloud, "This is my delighted Son, no, this is my beloved Son. Hear Him." And then they went down the mountain and Jesus told them not to tell anyone because it was a secret. That's it!

Late April
David and the Temple
By Sharon

Every time I have to think, think, think. David and his son ... One day when David was in his palace sitting, he was thinking about God and he said he wanted to build a beautiful house for God. So he went to Nathan and told him if he can make a house for God. And Nathan said it was a good idea without asking God. And then he went to his palace. And then God told Nathan that David cannot build the house. He could only make the stuff to build it. God told Nathan that his son had to build it. And then David died and his son went to build the house and then the people saw it and they worshipped God a lot.

No doubt some of children's improvement in language (and ability to use story structure) is due to maturation and some is the result of activities at home and school. Language development is a complex process, and in general classroom practice over a year's time, it is extremely difficult if not impossible to separate all the strands. We've all seen television commercials promoting a particular cereal as part of a balanced, healthful breakfast. They can't claim that the product

9

they're advertising is the answer to all your nutritional needs, but they can say that it contributes to a larger goal. Providing children with opportunities like retelling in which they use focused, lengthy speech makes sense intuitively.

After taking a statistics course in graduate school, I was required to do a research project using what I'd learned. I compared one of the retellings that my class had done at the beginning of the year with one they did at the end of the year. Predictably, they showed significant improvement. Was it the result of maturation or of practice with retelling? Next I compared our second retelling with the same story done by a class at a nearby school at the same time of year. My class scored significantly higher. Logically, to me at least, this made perfect sense. I interpreted their scores to mean that their repeated retelling practice was responsible for the difference. One of the professors who taught language arts courses gently suggested that it might be the result of a combination of many language-rich activities rather than just one. At the time I didn't want to hear that, but now I agree. Think back to Roberto's and Michelle's stories in chapter 1. These were dictated at the end of the year and were only the third or fourth retelling the class had done. Yet they are just as good as those done by some of my other classes who had done retelling all year. Retelling is one part of a language-rich environment that supports the development of vocabulary and language complexity; by itself, it isn't the answer to all your students' language development needs. Any language improvement that results from the use of retelling is a combination of several elements:

- **Adult modeling of correct and more complex language.** Notice the incorrect pronoun use by Bethany in all but one phrase—a line she remembered from the story. Over the next six weeks, she gradually did self-correction until she was consistently using pronouns correctly:

Part of the Creation Story
By Bethany

Jesus made the peoples an' Jesus made da amals and Jesus made the church. Him lie down. Him rested because Him was all done. That doesn't mean He was tired, it mean it was to show all the people to lie down.

- **The stressing of certain linguistic patterns.** Note how the language changes at the part in the story where Patty incorporates the memory verse:

Triumphal Entry
By Patty

Once upon a time Jesus was going to Jerusalem and den one day He said, "Get a donkey." Dey found a donkey dat hadn't been used for years and dey took it to Jesus. And den when dey got der, all da people made a nice rug for Jesus. "Hosanna, blessed is He who comes in the name of the Lord!" People frew down der coats and children went to get fwowers and people waved palm tree branches and dey were so happy dat Jesus was der king.

- **Children's increased sense of structure in expository material or narratives.**

- **Extra practice and experience in focused, extended language use.**

There is a wealth of testimonial articles about how teachers—foreign language teachers, ESL teachers, special needs teachers—have successfully used retelling with their students. That doesn't mean that it is always easy for students. As Sharon said in her story about David and the temple, they have to "think, think, think," but with appropriate support they can experience success in retelling. In the following story, Julio, who'd been learning English for slightly over a year at this point, didn't worry about getting all the words right. He just plunged in with enthusiasm, a characteristic of young children that is part of the charm of using retelling in children's early years:

The Fiery Furnace
By Julio

Firs' their went to a other country an' at a en was a king an' den an' was a big fience an den da king said when da music starts you are gonna lan me. An' den he no wants to lan to da king an' at da 'en, "Soldiers! Come an' throw it in da fire!" An' den, "You frow free peoples in da fire." And den, "Der not crying! Der not dying! Der walking in da fire! I think Jesus is wis him." ["Fience" is probably furnace, and "lan" appears to be connected with bowing down or lying down on the land.]

Recall and Comprehension

For many of us, the term *recitation* (studying something and then reciting it back to demonstrate retention) conjures up images of quaint one-room schoolhouses on the frontier. For centuries it has been a widely used and accepted educational method for promoting learning, and it is still used in school systems around the world. Charlotte Mason's (1989) "narration" method modified the memory requirement from a word-for-word recital of the text to a detailed recounting of the

9

ideas presented in the material. The underlying belief in both is that it is important for students to be able to correctly recall information. While this can be an end in itself, thinking depends on a ready access to facts. Perhaps it was an end in itself at times, but it also provided ready access to facts, the raw materials for thinking.

Recall, however, isn't the only benefit of verbal rehearsal when more than lists are involved. We've probably all had the experience of solving a problem by "talking it out"—either with a friend or by ourselves when we're alone. Sometimes making a problem explicit through speech helps us understand the situation. Have you ever been with a friend who poured out her heart, decided what to do about the situation, and then thanked you for your help, when all you did was listen? Simply saying or reading something aloud often promotes comprehension of the material.

Recall and comprehension provide the raw material for application, particularly when we are dealing with Bible stories. We weave together the story and its application, the memory verse and appropriate life applications of it, songs that support recall and application, and work sheets, artwork, or crafts that support application—all surrounded by prayer—with the goal of having children form a deep and lasting relationship with God. Retelling doesn't ensure that this goal will be reached, but it plays a part. Note that the concept about God's ability to provide is grounded in the following story:

9

God Provides for His People
By Winton

Once upon a time Moses tried to lead the people out of the country where the king Pharoah was. He took them out to the desert where there wasn't enough food. They told Moses that they didn't have enough food. And Moses say to God, "I don't have enough food for these people." But God said, "I do." And early the next morning the people found some little things like crackers. "That's what God has sent you." Then they took their bags and picked it up and put it in their bags. And in the night God told them to eat what he sended what was called quail. And the people called those little crackers things manna. And the people said, "Moses, we're thirsty." And God told Moses to get a stick and hit a rock and all of a sudden there was water coming out and there was a big lake almost like a river.

Personal Responsibility and Focused Attention

Ensuring that your students know before you start that they will be retelling expository material or a story encourages them to focus their attention, thereby taking responsibility for their learning. Some children will drift along in group settings unless they are engaged verbally or physically. It may be that they are unaccustomed to attending closely when someone speaks in front of a group or that language differences make sustained attention difficult. If you've ever tried to listen for an extended period of time when the speaker used a language unfamiliar to you, you can sympathize.

One year we read the same unfamiliar fable to children in six classes (prekindergarten through fourth grade). All the teachers except the second-grade teacher, who forgot to mention it, told the children that

9

they would each be retelling the fable later. As you might expect, the scores increased with age, reflecting the children's growing familiarity with story structure and language complexity. This upward trend in scores held in all class results except for those of the second-grade class. The graphs looked as if someone had punched them with a fist where the second-grade results were recorded. It's not a surprising result, I suppose. We all listen more carefully when we know the material "will be on the test."

The desire to feel a part of the group prompts some children to take on more responsibility for their learning. I found that students who were content to give the answer "I don't know" when asked to retell a story at the beginning of the year realized fairly quickly that their peers were able to say something (sometimes very little, but something). They began paying closer attention so that they too could share something when it was their turn.

Another incentive involves asking students for permission to read their work aloud to the class and praising specific parts of it. You don't have to read everyone's story every time, but make sure that you share this honor with all the class members during the year. Choose one or two stories each time to spotlight. As you compliment the class on their listening and retelling, casually mention that you would like to read one or two stories aloud to the class if their authors would allow you to do so. To focus the students' attention, find something specific to praise in the retelling. ("Julio told the story like a story; his voice was excited at the exciting parts. When we write, we can show that by using this mark—! [Show the exclamation mark to the students.] Do you see where I used it in his story to show how excited his voice was? See? Here and here and here. Thank you, Julio, for letting me read your story.") Sometimes it is a challenge to find something to praise,

9

but usually, if you supported the child enough during the retelling, there is something. Find it, praise him, and he will keep trying.

Interestingly, at times some students would ask for a brief review of the main points of the story immediately after they'd heard it in order to fix the story in their minds. They might be the ones to supply the three or four main points of the story during that review, showing that they knew them all along, but they took the responsibility for reinforcing their memory. I've already mentioned that a few took the initiative of asking me to reread what I'd just typed so that they could make sure they were happy with it.

A Sense of Accomplishment

In general, children feel a sense of accomplishment and pride over having their words in print, available for all to read. I hadn't realized how much pride some students took in their work until one parent told me that when they were packing to return to the United States and her daughter had to choose which of her most prized possessions to fit in the small backpack she would carry on the plane, one of her choices was her book of stories.

Benefits for Teachers

Teaching is an art rather than a mechanical series of decisions. Good teachers instinctively keep one eye on the subject matter and the other on their students' learning. These teachers reflect on their practice and their effectiveness, and they modify their teaching accordingly. Encouraging all teachers to do this has become standard practice.

9

For teachers, one of the key benefits of retelling is that it provides them with the raw material to gauge how a student is grasping what they are teaching. As adults we have forgotten much of how the world looks to young children. Children's experiences or lack of them may influence how the children interpret what we say even though we may not realize it. Narratives by children often provide insight into how those children are thinking—in a way that their answers to specific questions do not.

I found the retellings to be an extremely rich, informal assessment measure of student understanding and learning. Some children needed hints or helps to get going and recall details, and that was fine. At times asking them additional questions was necessary to gain a more complete picture of their comprehension. Their personal touches never failed to entertain me. In the following story by Daric, the phrase "God is gonna take his soul away" sounds like part of a bedtime prayer, and he includes a little Bolivian twist at the end. (In his culture, it was common to send notes or packages to another home with a trusted taxi driver.) As I said earlier, the children's stories never sounded exactly like mine, and that was what made them so interesting to me:

David and Saul
By Daric

Once upon a time a king very nasty lived in a place an' den somebody came to da tell him dey God is gonna take his soul away an' den he got angry an' den he got sad. An' den he was throwing things to people an' a servant came an' tell to David to bring someting to make 'em happy. And then he got ready an' he talk who is gonna take care of da sheep. An' then he went and the king was still throwing things an' den

9

he sit down an' den he played the music an' da king stopped throwing things an' breaking things. Den he said, "Why don't you come to play that music every day?" An' then he said to a man to call a taxi an' go an' send a note to his father of David dat there aways an' he did an' he always played the music for the king.

In the following story, Patty includes information she learned from our science unit on food groups. It's interesting to see that she is in the process of self-correcting some of her lingering speech habits:

The Ten Plagues
By Patty

Pharoah, well he was really mean and he killed all the baby boys. And den what happened was he was really mean king. So God said, "Let my people go." And he said, "**No!**" So you know what? He sent frogs. But he still said no. And den what happened was He sent flies. And what happened was He made the cows very sick. Dey couldn't get any milk or ice cream. The Pharoah still said, "**No!**" So then He made a red lake and der was no fwesh water to dwink. But Pharoah still said, "**No!**" Den God said, "I know something that will really make you say yes this time." And den He told the people to kill a lamb and paint the blood on the door. And then they ate the lamb and ate fin bread and den the angel just passed over the doors wis blood. And then the oldest son in each family that didn't have blood on the door died. And den everyone was crying and Pharoah said, "Get out, people, and never come back again!"

I used children's retellings to help me evaluate and modify my teaching. Through it I realized that many figures of speech were completely lost on some children, perhaps because of their age or their limited English proficiency. I learned through experience rather than through theory that what I said was not transferred verbatim to their minds. Often there were major differences. They interpreted what I said in a way that made sense to them, given their experience, and sometimes it was not so much in the words as in the tone that I caught the mistakes.

One of my earliest attempts at recording retellings involved the story of David and Goliath. I told the story in a form that I thought would be understandable to my students. ("He cursed him by his gods" became something like "Goliath said terrible things to David.") When my students retold the story, they caught the idea that Goliath said bad things to David. And they faithfully retold the part about David using a stone and a sling to kill Goliath. What I was unprepared for was their enthusiastic linking of the two ideas. The emphasis they placed on the first two words in the phrase "**And so** David picked up a rock," said with such gusto and sympathetic understanding, made me review the story with them the next day, carefully emphasizing that David did not throw rocks at Goliath because Goliath said bad things to him and that we are *not* to throw rocks at people because we don't like what they say.

I realized that some children totally missed the point of my examples, glossing over similes ("like") and explanations that were meant to clarify. When I attempted to give my class a mental picture of Lazarus and the long cloth strips that were wrapped around him, all the members of the class apparently understood—all, that is, except for Rony:

9

Jesus Raises Lazarus
By Rony

There two sisters and one man died. And then his sisters was crying. And then he was, and then he called Jesus and Jesus camed and Jesus came until the man died. And they put him, rolled him with toilet paper. And then Jesus came. He say, "Please God, help my best friend." And then he help him. And then the bad men say, "We have to keel Jesus. He can't make him heal sick. We keel him. We have to keel Jesus now." And that's all.

Another time, while telling the story of Noah, I wanted to give the children an idea of the length of time involved, so I told them that Noah was on the ark a long, long time, "like as long as from now until Christmas." The phrase "Noah was in the ark until Christmas" found its way into several retellings. Over time I became more careful when I told stories so as to prevent misunderstandings.

Leaving the lofty thoughts of becoming a better teacher behind, let's turn to the practical—to thoughts of cost. I've already mentioned that retelling activities can be costly in time, and obviously you must consider that aspect. Can you fit retelling into your schedule? Probably, if you want to. Retelling is flexible; you can use it and reuse it and reuse it again, each time differently, without buying anything new. Unless you have an unusually generous budget for supplies, that benefit should make you prick up your ears. Even if you try using retelling and decide to discard it later, how much have you lost?

One last benefit—not one that will stand up as a strong argument in a scholarly argument or that will convince those people who want numbers and test scores, but a benefit nevertheless—is in what retelling reveals. In this book I included stories as examples because of their charm; even now I smile as I read the words of those children and remember their faces. Kindergarten and the years surrounding it are a delightful time in a child's life. Retelling offers you the opportunity to catch a glimpse of the uniqueness of each child's thinking and personality and to preserve it.

Getting Started ...

Sometimes teachers get bored after a few years of teaching. Our curriculum guides dictate that we teach the same skills and the same material over and over, year after year. It's easy to get stuck in a rut and decide that it's time to teach a different grade, change schools, have a baby, retire—anything! Retelling is an antidote to that boredom because you're forever discovering more about people—very young people—as a group and as individuals.

Remember that in the first chapter I said that there is no one "right" way to do retelling? Obviously a teacher's personal philosophy and purpose will affect how and when (or even if) the teacher uses retelling. Some of us lean toward accepting whatever comes out of the minds and mouths of children and appreciating it as an expression of their individuality, and that's fine. Some of us feel the need to help them pay attention to details such as characters or setting to make their retellings more complete. That's fine, too. Related to this is whether or not you correct what children say. Some teachers would never interrupt a retelling, even to prompt; others prompt or cue to draw out more. Some correct misunderstandings on the spot; some allow them to stand or correct them later in a group setting. Some transcribe the children's words exactly as dictated; others clean them

9

up as they type. God made us each different; He has gifted us in different ways. As long as we ask for His guidance as we teach, act in love and respect toward the children that He has entrusted to us, and remember that we are accountable to Him, I think there is room for such differences.

Your purpose in using retelling will also make some ways of using it more attractive than others. Your primary reason may be to get a sense of whether your teaching is getting through or to build a sense of class togetherness through a shared retelling. If you are using it for review purposes, you may decide not to bother with recording it. On the other hand, if you plan to use it as a language assessment measure, you will take care to use a child's exact words and, perhaps, note the vocabulary or score it using T-units. If you are interested in a child's grasp of story structure or recall of the text, you may use a simple scoring method to note elements of story structure included in the retelling or in the details. Retelling is flexible enough for you to use in a wide variety of ways, depending on your students' development and abilities and on your aims.

I've offered you a variety of ideas as a springboard for your creativity. Some activities work with one group of children and not with another—anyone who has taught a few years knows that well. Pick one idea that you think you can use now—maybe something small— and try it several times. It takes time to determine what works for you. Modify the idea so that it fits with you and your children. Come up with other uses for retelling. Use your God-given creativity to bless your class. Enjoy the fascinating children He has given to you this year as you listen to them share their uniqueness through retelling.

Appendix: Resources on the Web

Book

Towards a Philosophy of Education, vol. 6, by Charlotte Mason, available online: http://www.amblesideonline.org/CM/toc.html#6

Vocabulary Lists

http://www.duboislc.org/EducationWatch/First100Words.html

http://www.manythings.org/vocabulary/lists/a/

http://en.wiktionary.org/wiki/Wiktionary:Frequency_lists

http://www.kidzone.ws/dolch/kindergarten.htm

http://www.psychwww.com/mtsite/forlangu.html#100Words

Graphic Organizers

http://www.edhelper.com/teachers/graphic_organizers.htm

http://www.writedesignonline.com/organizers/

http://www.region15.org/curriculum/graphicorg.html

Coloring Pages

http://www.christiananswers.net/kids/clr-indx.html

http://www.first-school.ws/theme/cp_bible.htm

http://www.coloring.ws/christian.htm

http://www.tstl.net/Children/Coloring/Coloring.asp

http://www.kids-corner.info/myintouch/youth/activities_people.html

http://free-coloring-pages.com/bible.html

Creating Flannel Board Backgrounds and Figures

http://www.flannelboardman.com/HOW%20TO%20MAKE%20
YOUR%20OWN%20FLANNEL%20BOARDS.htm

http://members.aol.com/Ivinsart/handbook.html

Kid Pix Computer Software

http://www.k12.hi.us/~mstlaure/tlcf2000/fun_kidpix.htm#draw

http://www.cap.nsw.edu.au/kidpix/kid_pix.html

http://www.edzone.net/~mwestern/KidPix/KPS.html

http://www.learningcompany.com/jump.
jsp?itemID=87&itemType=CATEGORY

Motions and Music CD

Let's Sing Motions 'n Music CD, available from Scripture Press (Cook
Ministries) as part of their preschool teaching resources packet:
http://www.davidccook.com/curriculum/scripturepress/index.cfm

References

Ausubel, D. P. 1960. The use of advance organizers in the learning and retention of meaningful verbal material. *Journal of Educational Psychology* 51:257–72.

Barrett, Ethel. 1960. *Storytelling—it's easy!* Grand Rapids, MI: Zondervan.

Blachowicz, Camille, and Donna Ogle. 2001. *Reading comprehension: Strategies for independent learners.* New York: Guilford Press.

Bower, Gordon H. 1976. Experiments on story understanding and recall. *Quarterly Journal of Experimental Psychology* 28, no. 4:511–34.

Brown, Hazel, and Brian Cambourne. 1987. *Read and retell.* Portsmouth, NH: Heinemann.

Brown, Marcia. 1947. *Stone soup.* New York: Aladdin Paperbacks.

Carroll, John B., Peter Davies, and Barry Richman. 1971. *American Heritage word frequency book.* Boston: Houghton Mifflin; New York: American Heritage Publishing.

Duke, Nell K. 2003. Information books in early childhood. *Beyond the Journal* (March). http://www.journal.naeyc.org/btj/200303/.

Gag, Wanda. 1928. *Millions of cats.* New York: Coward-McCann.

Gibson, Akimi, Judith Gold, and Charissa Sgouros. 2003. The power of story retelling. *The Tutor.* http://www.nwrel.org/learns/tutor/spr2003/spr2003.html.

Gladwell, Malcolm. 2000. *The tipping point: How little things can make a big difference.* Boston: Little Brown.

Goodman, Yetta M. 1982. Retellings of literature and the comprehension process. *Theory into Practice* 21, no. 4:301–8.

Hansen, Jill. 2004. *Tell me a story: Developmentally appropriate retelling strategies.* Newark, DE: International Reading Association.

Hart, Betty, and Todd R. Risley. 2003. The early catastrophe: The 30 million word gap by age 3. *American Educator* (Spring). http://www.aft.org/pubs-reports/american_educator/spring2003/catastrophe.html.

Hayes, Donald P. 2003. A guide to the lexical analysis of natural texts using QLEX or QANALYSIS. Cornell University Sociology Technical Report Series #2003-1. http://www.soc.cornell.edu/hayes-lexical-analysis/lexguide2003.html.

Hayes, Donald P., and Margaret G. Ahrens. 1988. Vocabulary simplification for children: A special case of "motherese"? *Journal of Child Language* 15:395–410.

Hunt, Kellogg W. 1965. *Grammatical structures written at three grade levels.* NCTE Research Report No. 3. Champaign, IL: National Council of Teachers of English.

Isbell, Rebecca, Joseph Sobol, Liane Lindauer, and April Lowrance. 2004. The effects of storytelling and story reading on the oral language complexity and story comprehension of young children. *Early Childhood Education Journal* 32, no. 3:157–63.

Lay-Dopyera, Margaret, and John Dopyera. 1990. *Becoming a teacher of young children.* 4th ed. New York: McGraw-Hill.

Loban, Walter. 1966. *Problems in oral English: Kindergarten through grade nine.* NCTE Research Report No. 5. Champaign, IL: National Council of Teachers of English.

Ma, Liping. 1999. *Knowing and teaching elementary mathematics: Teachers' understanding of fundamental mathematics in China and the United States.* Mahwah, NJ: Lawrence Erlbaum Associates.

Mandler, Jean M. 1983. This week's citation classic. *Current Contents* 17 (April 25).

Mandler, Jean M., and Nancy S. Johnson. 1977. Remembrance of things parsed: Story structure and recall. *Cognitive Psychology* 9:111–51.

Martin, Bill, Jr. 1992. *Brown bear, brown bear, what do you see?* New York: Henry Holt.

Mason, Charlotte M. 1989. *A philosophy of education.* Wheaton, IL: Tyndale House.

McCloskey, Robert. 1948. *Blueberries for Sal.* New York: Viking Press.

Morrow, Lesley Mandel. 1985. Retelling stories: A strategy for improving young children's comprehension, concept of story structure, and oral language complexity. *Elementary School Journal* 85, no. 5:647–61.

———. 1990. Assessing children's understanding of story through their construction and reconstruction of narrative, in *Assessment for instruction in early literacy*, edited by Lesley Mandel Morrow and Jeffrey K. Smith. Englewood Cliffs, NJ: Prentice Hall.

Moss, Barbara. 2004. Teaching expository text structures through information trade book retellings. *Reading Teacher* 57, no. 8:710–18.

Nelson, Robin. 2003. *From egg to chicken.* Minneapolis, MN: Lerner Publications.

Potter, Beatrix. n.d. *The tale of Peter Rabbit.* New York: Frederick Warne.

Richman, Barry. 1971. The development of the Corpus. In Carroll, Davies, and Richman 1971.

Shedlock, Marie L. 1917. *The art of the story-teller.* New York: D. Appleton. http://digital.library.upenn.edu/women/shedlock/story/story.html.

Skouge, James R. 2004. *Pacific voices: Integrating multimedia, technology, and culture into education.* Honolulu, HI: Pacific Resources for Education and Learning.

Stead, Tony. 2002. *Is that a fact? Teaching nonfiction writing K–3.* Portland, ME: Stenhouse.

The Three Bears. 1965. Racine, WI: Western Publishing.

Yaden, David. 1988. Understanding stories through repeated read-alouds: How many does it take? *Reading Teacher* 41, no. 6:556–60.